SERIES EDITOR: JOHN MOORE

ORDER OF BATTLE SERIES: 5

THE ARDENNES OFFENSIVE

U.S. V CORPS & XVIII (AIRBORNE) CORPS

NORTHERN SECTOR

BRUCE QUARRIE

First published in Great Britain in 1999 by Osprey Publishing,
Elms Court, Chapel Way, Botley, Oxford OX2 9LP
Email: osprey@osprey-publishng.co.uk

ISBN 1 85532 854 2

Osprey Series Editor: Lee Johnson
Ravelin Series Editor: John Moore
Research Co-ordinator: Diane Moore
Design: Ravelin Limited, Braceborough, Lincolnshire, United Kingdom
Cartography: Chapman Bounford and Associates, London, United Kingdom

Printed through Worldprint Ltd, Hong Kong

99 00 01 02 03 10 9 8 7 6 5 4 3 2 1

FOR A CATALOGUE OF ALL BOOKS PUBLISHED BY OSPREY MILITARY,
AUTOMOTIVE AND AVIATION PLEASE WRITE TO:

The Marketing Manager, Osprey Direct UK, P.O. Box 140,
Wellingborough, Northants, NN8 4ZA United Kingdom

The Marketing Manager, Osprey Direct USA,
P.O. Box 130, Sterling Hts, MI 48311-0130, USA

VISIT THE OSPREY WEBSITE AT:
http://www.osprey-publishing.co.uk

Series style

The style of presentation adopted in the Order of Battle series is designed to
provide quickly the maximum information for the reader.

Order of Battle Unit Diagrams – All 'active' units in the ORBAT, that is those
present and engaged on the battlefield are shown in black. Unengaged and
detached units, as well as those covered in subsequent volumes are
'shadowed'.

Unit Data Panels – These provide a ready reference for all regiments,
battalions, companies and troops forming part of each division or battlegroup
and present during the battle, together with dates of attachment where relevant.

Battlefield Maps – In this volume, German units are shown in red and Allied
units in blue.

Order of Battle Timelines

Battle Page Timelines – Each volume concerns the Order of Battle for the
armies involved. Rarely are the forces available to a commander committed
into action as per his ORBAT. To help the reader follow the sequence of events,
a Timeline is provided at the bottom of each 'battle' page. This Timeline gives
the following information:

The top line bar defines the actual time of the actions being described in that
battle section.

The middle line shows the time period covered by the whole action.

The bottom line indicates the page numbers of the other, often interlinked,
actions covered in this book.

0800 hrs	0900	1000	1100	1200
	pp45-47	48-49 & 52-55	50-51	

Key to Military Series symbols

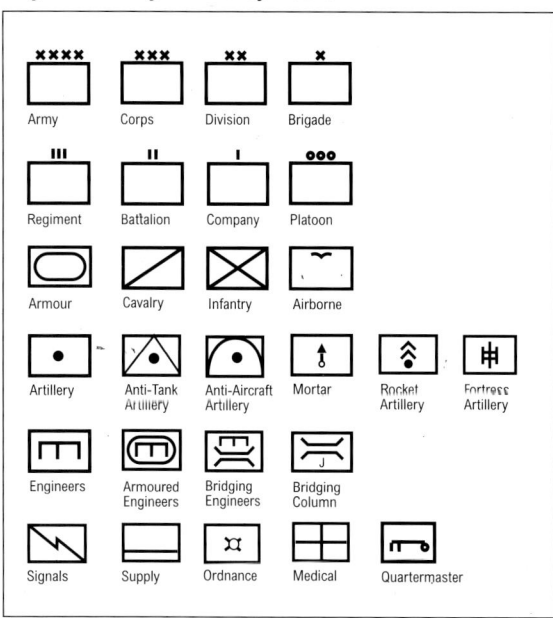

Army — Corps — Division — Brigade

Regiment — Battalion — Company — Platoon

Armour — Cavalry — Infantry — Airborne

Artillery — Anti-Tank Artillery — Anti-Aircraft Artillery — Mortar — Rocket Artillery — Fortress Artillery

Engineers — Armoured Engineers — Bridging Engineers — Bridging Column

Signals — Supply — Ordnance — Medical — Quartermaster

Author's acknowledgements

This book would not have been possible without the generous support of Bob
Kane, Chairman of Presido Press, Novato, California for supplying and permitting
the use of material from Shelby L. Stanton's landmark book *World War II Order of
Battle* (1984).

Editor's note

All individual battle maps are based on Government Survey 1:50,000 G.S. 4040
series dated 1938 and 1939, revised from aerial reconnaissance 1943, by
permission of The British Library.

CONTENTS

DESTINATION BERLIN

Advance to the West Wall

By December 1944, the Allied forces had achieved an extraordinary amount since D-Day, but fallen far short of the 'home by Christmas' ideal. The Germans were, for the most part, still securely entrenched behind the 'Siegfried Line' (West Wall) and, far from giving up the struggle, were fighting more fiercely than ever now that they were on their own soil. The 'final push' would have to wait until the New Year but then, everyone outside Berlin agreed, it *would* be over by Christmas.

In the meanwhile, the self-appointed Führer of Nazi Germany had a surprisingly nasty seasonal gift planned which would give everyone heartburn and headaches, but not from festive cheer.

When the Allied American, British and Canadian troops stormed ashore in Normandy on 6 June, the end of the European war seemed firmly in sight. Confidence was enormous, especially with the Soviets pressing forward so vigorously in the east. Establish a beachhead, break out quickly, then a lightning thrust

through the industrial heartland of Germany in the Ruhr and on to the ultimate goal, Berlin. But the fates dictated otherwise, in more ways than one.

The long and careful planning which had gone into operation 'Overlord' had proved its value. The deception scheme intended to convince the Germans that the invasion would come in the Pas de Calais had been successful in keeping them uncertain, with the result that their coastal defence regiments were thinly stretched. Only at 'Omaha' was the resistance really fierce, and the Allies were rapidly able to consolidate

SHAEF (Supreme Headquarters' Allied Expeditionary Force). From left to right: Lieutenant-General Omar N. Bradley, Admiral Sir Bertram Ramsey, Air Chief Marshal Sir Arthur Tedder, General Dwight D. Eisenhower, General Sir Bernard Montgomery, Air Chief Marshal Sir Trafford Leigh-Mallory and Lieutenant-General Walter Bedell Smith.
(Imperial War Museum, London)

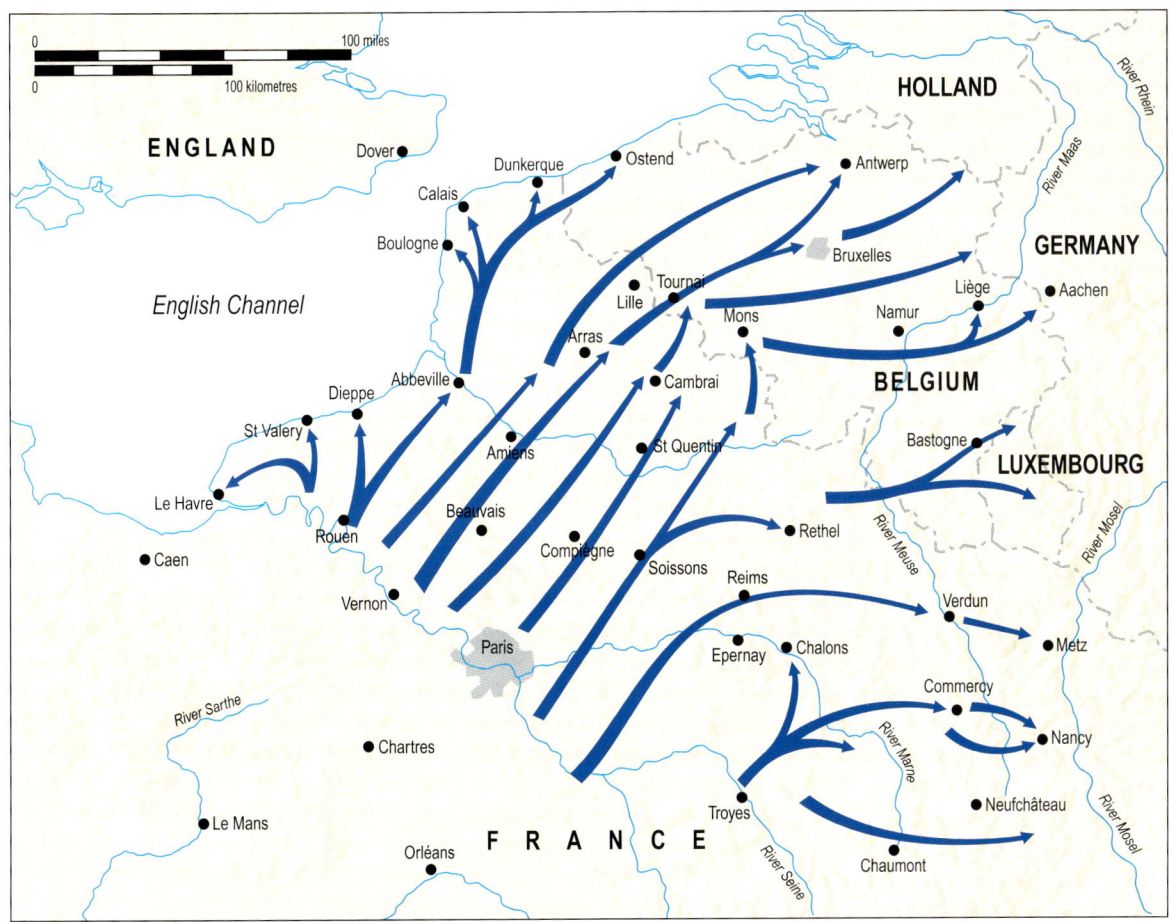

The 'broad front' strategy proposed by Bradley after the breakout from Normandy was accepted by SHAEF in preference to Montgomery's narrower, more north-easterly thrust towards the Ruhr, the heartland of German industry.

their precarious foothold on the continent and begin moving inland to make room on the beaches for the tens of thousands of men and vehicles which followed the first wave.

Initial progress was thus encouraging but, despite the Allies' vast aerial supremacy, the Germans succeeded in getting several Panzer divisions into Normandy which counter-attacked desperately, especially in the Caen sector, which slowed the British advance. Similarly, on their right the American divisions could only struggle almost inch by inch through the dense hedgerows of the bocage. In the north, Montgomery launched two major operations against Caen, 'Epsom' and 'Goodwood', but the defence did not really begin to crumble until the American First Army, having finally captured St Lô, could launch operation 'Cobra' and break out from the Cotentin

peninsula through Avranches, fanning right into Brittany and left to link up with the British and Canadians and cut off the bulk of the Panzer divisions in the Falaise pocket. Even this was not accomplished easily because a determined, if ill-conceived, counter-attack at Mortain did delay Bradley's advance.

After Patton's Third Army got ashore, Bradley assumed command of the United States' 12th Army Group while Courtney Hodges took over First Army; Montgomery remained in command of the British Second and Canadian First Armies which constituted 21st Army Group, and he was to prove an embarrassment to Eisenhower by constantly demanding that he be given back overall command of all operations on the ground. This was a rift which would be reopened during the Ardennes campaign.

The two Army Group commanders each had their own ideas as to how the campaign should be conducted now they had broken out of Normandy. Montgomery favoured a northerly straight-line thrust while Bradley believed in a broader drive to the east which would link up with Patch's Seventh Army after it had landed on the Mediterranean coast in August.

In the end Eisenhower came down in Bradley's favour, not because he was a fellow American, but because it was vital to get one or more of the major Channel ports reopened.

In addition to advancing east, therefore, Bradley's forces were assigned St Malo, Brest and Lorient, while Montgomery was to assault Le Havre, Dieppe, Boulogne, Calais and, the ultimate goal, the vast port of Antwerp whose facilities on their own could supply all the Allies' needs. Unfortunately, all of the ports were stubbornly defended; some, such as Lorient, never did fall and only surrendered at the end of the war; and those which were captured were in ruins, partly as a result of the Allied air, land and sea bombardment, and partly as a result of German demolition.

The failure to capture a port intact at an early stage of the campaign brought exactly the result which Eisenhower had feared. After the fall of Paris, while Montgomery struggled north up the coast of France and Belgium, Bradley's forces fanned out eastward and advanced rapidly against an enemy who seemed to be melting away and only offering real resistance at occasional natural choke points. The speed of the advance meant that supplies, especially of fuel and ammunition, were taking longer and longer to reach the front line divisions, and eventually in September the inevitable happened: they ran out of fuel completely. The 7th Armored Division, for example, was stranded for four whole days. This gave the Germans an invaluable breathing space in which to reinforce their West Wall and withdraw divisions to Holland and Germany to rest, re-equip and have their casualties replaced in readiness for the Ardennes campaign which was already being planned.

The Allied plan for the beginning of 1945 was for Ninth Army to drive towards Duisburg and Düsseldorf, First Army towards Köln and Bonn, and Third Army towards Saarbrücken. The German offensive caused all three to be postponed.

It was in this environment that Montgomery conceived the idea of seizing a crossing over the lower Rhine at Arnhem by dropping paratroop divisions to seize the necessary bridges in Holland and create a road along which an armoured corps could break through then turn east towards the Ruhr. Unfortunately, II SS-Panzer Korps was one of the formations pulled out of the line for the Ardennes offensive, and it was resting and refitting outside Arnhem, so Montgomery's plan failed. There is, perhaps, irony in the fact that it was the two U.S. airborne divisions involved in 'Market Garden', themselves recuperating outside Reims, France, in December 1944, which helped create a second 'bridge too far', but this time for the Germans.

Following the failure of the Arnhem operation, the Allies resumed their 'broad front' strategy which resulted in the costly siege of Aachen – the first major German town to succumb – followed by the slow but inexorable advance to the West Wall and the River Rur, the last natural and man-made obstacles west of the Rhine. However, it was behind just these defences that Adolf Hitler was mustering the forces for his last great gamble of the war on the western front, and the Allies' planned attacks towards Köln and Saarbrücken had to be postponed.

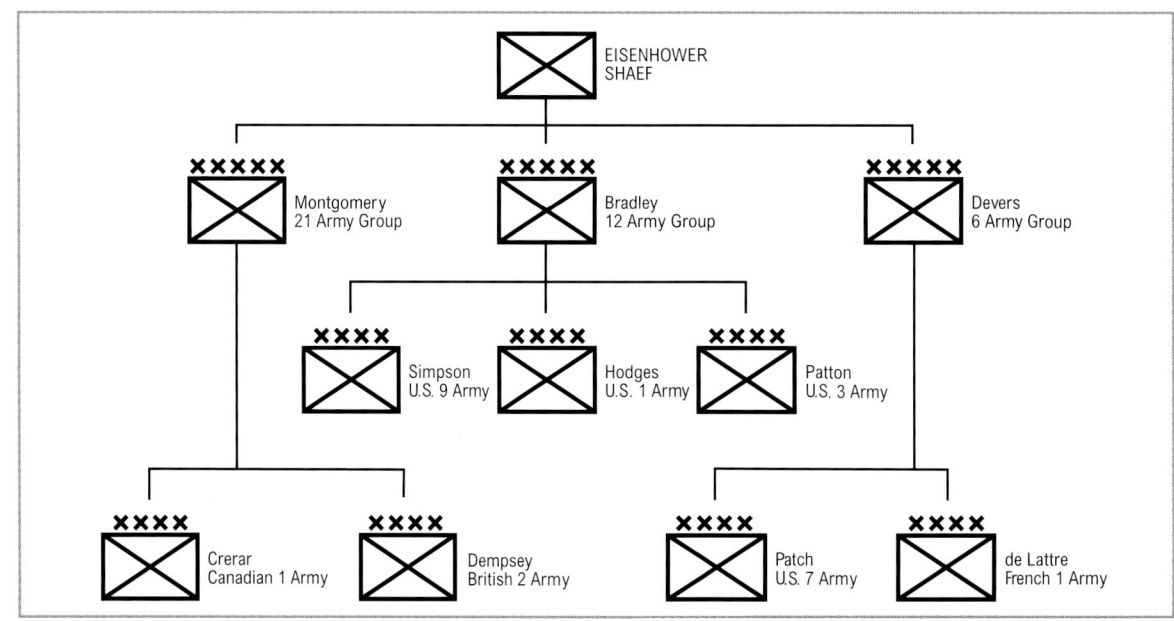

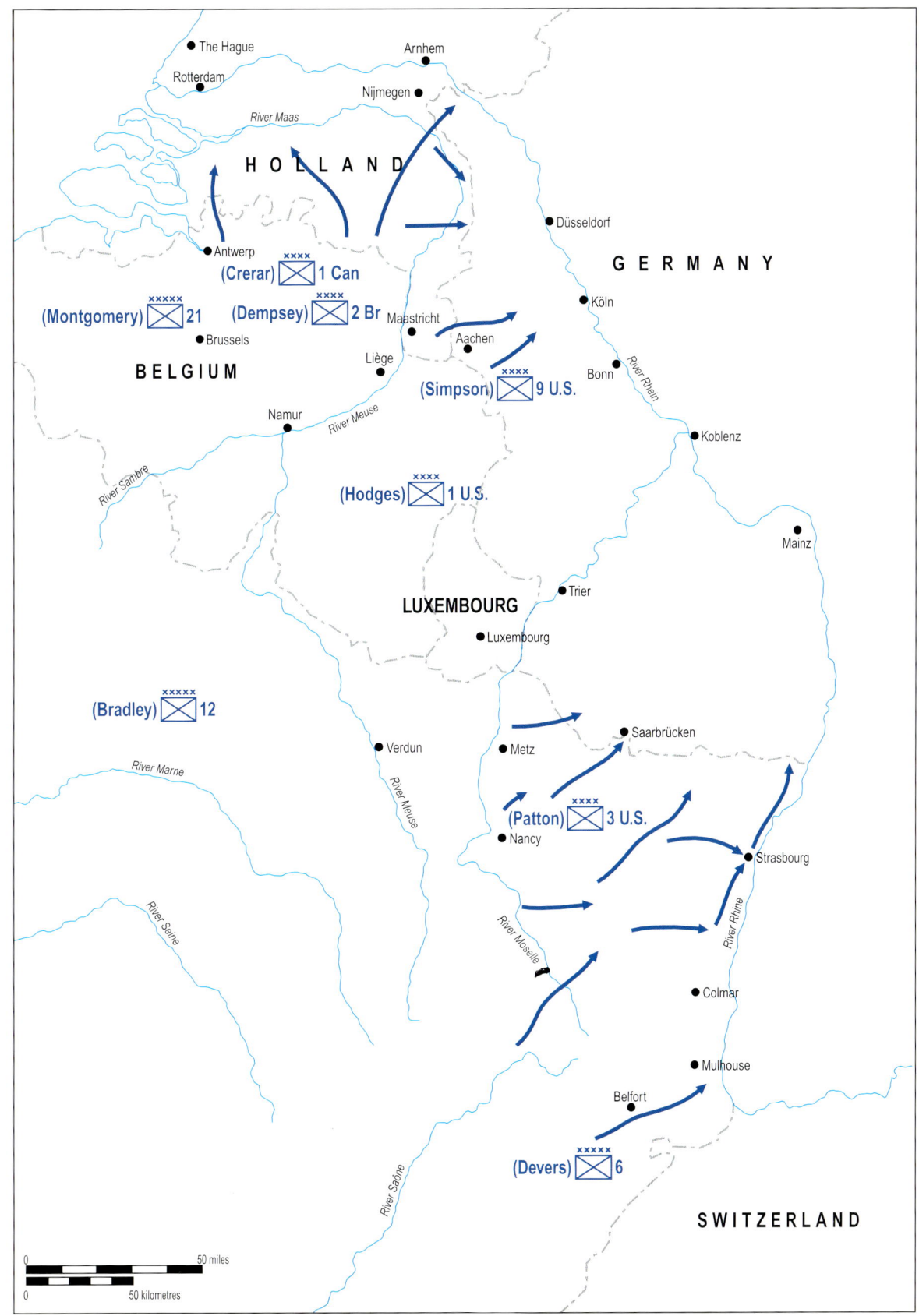

The Hague
Rotterdam
Arnhem
Nijmegen
River Maas
H O L L A N D
Düsseldorf
G E R M A N Y
Antwerp
(Crerar) 1 Can
Köln
(Montgomery) 21
(Dempsey) 2 Br
Maastricht
Aachen
Bonn
River Rhein
Brussels
Liège
(Simpson) 9 U.S.
B E L G I U M
Namur
River Meuse
Koblenz
River Sambre
(Hodges) 1 U.S.
Mainz
LUXEMBOURG
Trier
Luxembourg
(Bradley) 12
Saarbrücken
Verdun
Metz
River Marne
(Patton) 3 U.S.
River Meuse
Nancy
Strasbourg
River Seine
River Rhine
Colmar
River Moselle
Mulhouse
Belfort
River Saône
(Devers) 6
SWITZERLAND

0   50 miles

0   50 kilometres

THE BATTLE OF THE BULGE

Tackling the Crisis

Major-General (later, Sir) Kenneth Strong was Dwight Eisenhower's choice as SHAEF's Chief of Intelligence, and he has never sought excuses for the failure of Allied intelligence to detect the German build-up for what the C-in-C of Heeresgruppe B, Feldmarschall Walter Model, codenamed 'Herbstnebel' ('Autumn Mist'). Strong's book, *Intelligence at the Top*, was unfortunately written before the wraps were taken off 'Ultra', and evidence from this source – or the lack of it at this point in time due to German countermeasures – is carefully concealed in his narrative (which was, of course,

General Omar N. Bradley had been commander of II Corps in Sicily and First Army in Normandy before the creation of 12th Army Group.
(U.S. Signal Corps)

intelligence had relied on the radio interceptions of German messages using the 'Enigma' coding machine that, when the radios fell silent, they were at a loss.

Strong, who had begun his intelligence career as a subaltern in the British Army in Ireland during the 'Troubles' of 1916-17, spent two years in Berlin as a military attaché after Hitler's rise to power, and served as Allied Chief of Intelligence in North Africa, Sicily and Italy from 1942, was no novice at the 'spying game', and at the beginning of December had told SHAEF that 'the enemy's hand is dealt for a showdown before Christmas'. Eisenhower, he recalls, had expressed a

Major-General Kenneth Strong, Eisenhower's head of intelligence, had warned of the possibility of a German attack in the Ardennes.
(U.S. Signal Corps)

checked by the censor under the Official Secrets Act before publication). Thus Strong could only write that, when questioned by Eisenhower, he 'expressed concern about the difficulty of obtaining precise information on the unlocated German divisions, and also about the meaning of the constant movements of other divisions into and out of the Ardennes area'.

That the Germans were moving troops and equipment around behind the quiet Ardennes sector of the front towards the end of 1944 was no secret to the Allies. What was baffling was its relevance. What were the Germans up to? Allied intelligence was temporarily in the situation of a man suddenly struck blind, fumbling around in a once-familiar room now turned into an alien world. For so long, British and American

similar doubt when the two of them drove through the Ardennes (date unspecified), commenting on the danger of a 'nasty little Kasserine'.

At this point in early December 1944 the Allies were poised for two major offensives: the first by Major-General William Simpson's Ninth Army towards the Ruhr and the second by Major-General George Patton's Third Army towards the Saar. These fell north and south of the Ardennes, entrusted to Major-General Courtney Hodges' First Army, which was regarded as a 'quiet' zone to which troops freshly arrived in Europe could be assigned to get acclimatised, and in which those badly mauled in the earlier fighting around Aachen and in the Hürtgen Forest could recuperate. It was strongly felt that many

The battle for Aachen, the first major German town to fall into Allied hands, was a nightmare for the infantry of both sides, with an individual battle for practically every house and street corner often involving vicious hand-to-hand combat.
(U.S. Signal Corps)

German movements east of the Ardennes were for similar reasons, but even so, there was little complacency.

Allied intelligence, headed by Strong, was aware that several crack German divisions had, to all intents and purposes, 'disappeared'. That they were being rejuvenated for *something* was certain. But what? Strong himself said that such a reserve 'might be used for one of three purposes: first, it could be sent to the Russian front where pressure was great and where things were going badly for the Germans; secondly, it might be used to counter-attack a successful Allied penetration of the German front; thirdly, it might be used to launch a relieving attack through the Ardennes.' On the whole, Strong concluded – with the concurrence of both Bradley's and Montgomery's own intelligence staffs – that the second course was the most likely. They believed that Gerd von Rundstedt was in charge on the other side, and the old Field Marshal was known to be both cautious and predictable. Thus, since the directions of the next Allied offensives were clear to any schoolchild with an atlas, von Rundstedt could be expected to create reserves with which to oppose them.

What Allied intelligence completely failed to take into account was that the totally unpredictable mind of Adolf Hitler was, in fact, running the show, not the brain of von Rundstedt. Thus, although an attack through the Ardennes was not totally unexpected, the size of it came as a total surprise (despite claims in a recent book that Eisenhower deliberately left his centre weak in order to lure the enemy into a trap).

If the Allies *had* known the attack was impending, they would not have committed their armoured reserves to other operations, such as the drive to capture the Rur and Urft dams for example, which was launched on 13 December as a preliminary to Ninth Army's attack on the Ruhr scheduled for the New Year. And when the news did start filtering back, the initial reaction at the top was largely one of disbelief that the threat was real.

Eisenhower had called a meeting at SHAEF headquarters in Versailles for 1400 hrs on 16 December, at which both Strong and Omar Bradley were present. They were interrupted by Strong's deputy, Brigadier-General Thomas Betts, with news that reports were coming in of a series of 'strong and extensive attacks' against the American front in the Ardennes.

Looking at the map, Eisenhower felt sure they were driving for the Meuse and perhaps beyond that, to Bruxelles, but Bradley was initially sceptical. At 51 years of age, he had more first-hand experience of the Germans than Eisenhower, having been the latter's 'eyes and ears' in North Africa at the time of Kasserine Later he commanded first II Corps in Sicily and then First Army in Normandy before being promoted and given responsibility for 12th Army Group. Although unostentatious, he was a career professional and believed that, in von Rundstedt, he was facing an alter ego who would not indulge in anything rash. These German attacks, he said, could only be a spoiling move in reaction to First Army's offensive towards the Rur and Urft dams.

Eisenhower was not so sanguine and when, later in the afternoon, it became clear that at least eight German divisions were involved in the attack, Bradley at last telephoned Ninth Army commander William Simpson and ordered him to get 7th Armored Division moving south. Later he also alerted 3rd Armored and ordered George Patton to send 10th Armored as well. Bradley still remained unconvinced until, late that evening, an unexpected 'Ultra' intercept alerted SHAEF to the move of the Luftwaffe's II Jagdkorps, 'to support the attack of 5 and 6 Armies'. This really put the cat amongst the pigeons, because these two armies had been believed to be in the Bonn-Köln region. Bradley hurried back to his forward headquarters in Luxembourg city next morning a worried man.

U.S. INFANTRY DIVISION

(c. 14,000 men)

Division HQ & HQ Company

(3 x 57mm M1 anti-tank gun, 3 x .50 cal HMG, 6 x 2.36" M9A1 rocket-launcher [bazooka])

plus Military Police Platoon (c. 260 men)

INFANTRY REGIMENT (x 3)
(c. 3,200 men)
HQ Company (5 x .50 HMG & 7 x bazooka) (c.100 men)

I Battalion (c. 860 men)
HQ Company (3 x 57mm M1, 2 x .50 HMG, 2 x .30 HMG &
2 x 2.36" bazooka)
A, B & C Companies (each 2 x 81mm mortar, 3 x 60mm
mortar, 2 x . 50 HMG, 2 x . 30 HMG, 2 x .30 LMG & 9 x
bazooka)

II Battalion (c. 860 men)
HQ Company (as above)
D, E & F Companies (as above)

III Battalion (c. 860 men)
HQ Company (as above)
G, H & I Companies (as above) (no 10th-12th Companies)

13th Company (6 x 105mm M2A1 howitzer, 3 x .50 HMG &
9 x bazooka)
14th Company (6 x 57mm M1, 3 x .50 HMG & 9 x bazooka)

MEDIUM ARTILLERY BATTALION, 155m M1A1 (tractor-drawn)
(c. 530 men)
HQ Company (10 x bazooka)
A, B & C Batteries (each 4 x M1A1, 7 x .50 HMG &
10 x bazooka)

FIELD ARTILLERY BATTALION, 105m M2A1 (truck-drawn) (x 3)
(c. 520 men)
HQ Company (10 x bazooka)
A, B & C Batteries (each 4 x M2A1, 7 x .50 HMG &
10 x bazooka)

RECONNAISSANCE TROOP, MECHANIZED (c. 250 men)
(13 x M8 armoured car, 5 x M3 half-track, 3 x .50 HMG &
5 x bazooka)

ENGINEER COMBAT BATTALION (c. 640 men)
HQ Company (2 x bazooka)
A, B & C Companies (each 4 x .50 HMG, 6 x .30 LMG &
9 x bazooka)

MEDICAL BATTALION (c. 460 men)
HQ Company
A, B & C Companies (each 10 x fl-ton ambulance)

SIGNAL COMPANY (c. 220 men)
(6 x .50 HMG & 5 x bazooka)

QUARTERMASTER COMPANY (c. 190 men)
(59 trucks, 13 x .50 HMG & 5 x bazooka)

ORDNANCE LIGHT MAINTENANCE COMPANY (c. 140 men)
(5 x .50 HMG & 5 x bazooka)

ANTI-AIRCRAFT ARTILLERY AUTO-WEAPONS BATTALION
(c. 830 men) (attached one per division)
HQ Company
A, B & C Batteries (each 8 x 37mm M1A2 or
40mm Bofors & 8 x .50 HMG)

TANK BATTALION (c. 740 men) (attached one or two
per division)
HQ Company (2 x M4 Sherman [75mm])
A, B & C Companies (each 17 x M4 [75mm] &
2 x M4 [105mm])
D Company (17 x M5 Stuart or M24 Chaffee)

TANK DESTROYER BATTALION (c. 700 men) (attached one
or two per division)
HQ Company (6 x M8)
A, B & C Companies (each 12 x GMC, predominantly M10
with some M18/M36)

Closer to the front line, at his own headquarters in Spa, First Army commander Courtney Hicks Hodges had, like Eisenhower, reacted instinctively to the new threat on his front, taking CCB of 9th Armored Division away from temporary attachment to V Corps and sending it towards St Vith, and a regiment from 1st Infantry Division towards Elsenborn. Although taciturn, with a pessimistic manner, Hodges was highly respected by both his superiors at SHAEF and liked by the men under his command, because he always showed concern for their welfare. But Hodges, almost alone amongst the American 'top brass', had seen combat as a company commander during World War 1, and knew what it was like at the 'sharp end'.

By the third day of the German offensive, a much clearer picture of the threat had emerged and a great deal had been done to stabilise the front, although it was too late to save two whole regiments of the 106th Infantry Division of VIII Corps from being surrounded and forced to surrender. XVIII (Airborne) Corps had been released from SHAEF reserve to reinforce Bastogne in the south and block Kampfgruppe 'Peiper' in the north; and fresh infantry divisions, such as the 75th which had arrived in Europe only days before, were also being thrown into the affray. This, then, was the situation when Eisenhower called Bradley, Patton and other senior officers including the commander of 6th Army Group, Lieutenant-General Jacob Devers, to

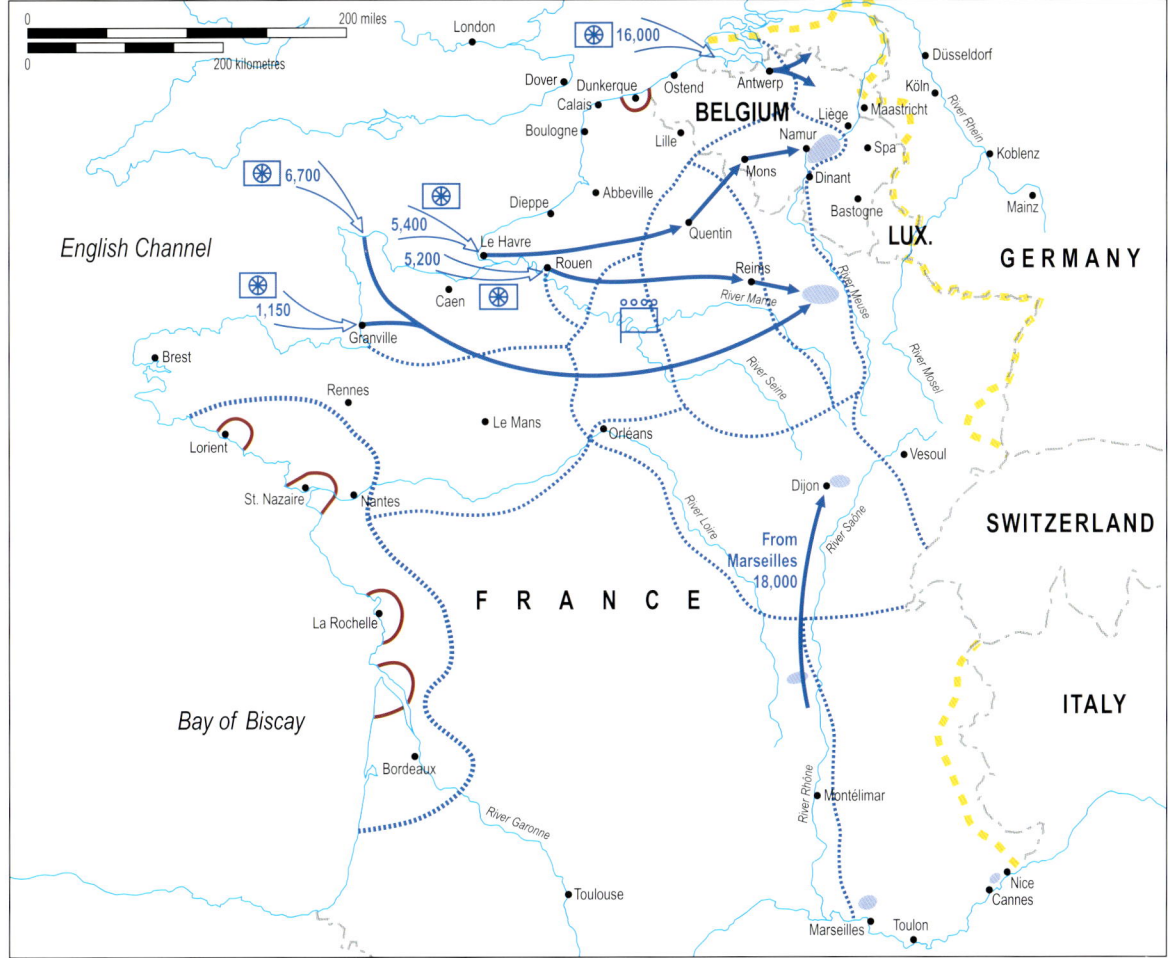

As the Allies advanced further to the east (the front line is in orange), they outstretched their supply lines (shown in blue, leading to their major supply depots, also in blue). By the middle of December 1944 though, some of the Channel ports (shown here with supplies delivered in tons) were functioning again. German garrisons continued to resist around Lorient, St. Nazaire, La Rochelle and Dunkerque though.

a meeting at Bradley's rear headquarters in Verdun. The question was, if Devers shifted some of his weight north to reinforce Third Army, could Patton shift III Corps to reinforce Bastogne? (His XII Corps was already in action against Brandenberger's Seventh Armee on the southern flank of the offensive.) 'Hell, yes,' said Patton. 'When can you start?' asked Eisenhower. 'As soon as you're through with me.' And he was almost as good as his word. Later that day a new actor stepped on to the stage: Field Marshal Sir Bernard Law Montgomery. While Eisenhower had been in conference in Verdun, his deputy chief of operations, Major-General John 'Jock' Whiteley, had

received a telephone call from the commander of the Anglo-Canadian 21st Army Group suggesting that Eisenhower put him in command of all Allied forces north of 'the bulge'. Late that evening the proposal was put to Eisenhower, who said he would discuss it in the morning. However, 'Ike' had not been selected as Allied Supreme Commander for nothing. Walking over to his map, he considered Montgomery's suggestion. The two men did not enjoy an easy relationship, because Eisenhower had already experienced the Field Marshal's inflated sense of self-importance. Could this be another of Monty's manoeuvres to try to regain control of all ground forces in Europe, something he had been pushing for on and off for months?

Yet, as he looked at the map, Eisenhower quickly saw that the proposal had considerable merit. With communications between Bradley's forward headquarters in Luxembourg City and Hodges' new First Army HQ in Chaudfontaine being difficult, how could Bradley control the northern sector of the front effectively? Making up his mind, Eisenhower drew a

U.S. AIRBORNE DIVISION

(c. 11,000 men)

Division HQ & HQ Company (c. 200 men) plus Military Police and Reconnaissance Platoons

---

PARACHUTE INFANTRY REGIMENT (x 2–5)
 (c. 1,950 men)
HQ Company (1 x .30 HMG) (c. 80 men)

I Battalion (c. 580 men)
HQ Company (1 x .30 HMG, 8 x .30 LMG, 1 x 81mm mortar &
 2 x bazooka)
A, B & C Companies (each 9 x .30 LMG, 1 x 81mm mortar,
 3 x 60mm mortar & 9 x bazooka)

II Battalion (as I Battalion)
HQ Company
D, E & F Companies

III Battalion (as I Battalion)
HQ Company
G, H & I Companies

GLIDER INFANTRY REGIMENT (x 2)
 (c. 2,000 men)
HQ Company (c. 80 men)
Anti-tank Company (8 x 37mm M3 & 8 x .30 HMG)

I Battalion (c. 600 men)
HQ Company (1 x 81mm mortar, 2 x 60mm mortar,
 1 x .50 HMG & 1 x .30 HMG)
A, B & C Companies (each 2 x 60mm mortar, 1 x .30 LMG &
 9 x bazooka)

II Battalion (as I Battalion)
HQ Company .
D, E & F Companies

III Battalion (as I Battalion)
HQ Company
G, H & I Companies

PARACHUTE FIELD ARTILLERY BATTALION (x 2) (c. 580 men)
HQ Company (3 x .50 HMG)
A, B & C Batteries (each 4 x 75mm M1A1 Pack Howitzer &
 5 x .50 HMG)
Anti-tank Company (4 x 37mm M3 & 5 x .50 HMG)

GLIDER FIELD ARTILLERY BATTALION (x 2) (c. 370 men)
HQ Company
A, B & C Batteries (each 4 x 75mm M1A1 & 3 x .50 HMG)

AIRBORNE ANTI-AIRCRAFT BATTALION (c. 500 men)
HQ Company
A, B & C Batteries (each 8 x 37mm M1A2 or 40mm Bofors &
 12 x .50 HMG)

AIRBORNE ENGINEER BATTALION (c. 400 men)
HQ Company (1 x .30 LMG & 5 x bazooka)
A & B Companies (each 5 x .30 LMG & 10 x bazooka)

AIRBORNE MEDICAL COMPANY (c. 210 men)
 (7 x handcart)

AIRBORNE SIGNAL COMPANY (c. 80 men)
 (1 x light truck, no heavy weapons)

AIRBORNE QUARTERMASTER COMPANY (c. 90 men)
(30 x light truck, no heavy weapons)

AIRBORNE ORDNANCE LIGHT MAINTENANCE COMPANY
 (c. 75 men)
 (2 x .50 HMG & 5 x bazooka)

---

line across the map and picked up his telephone. Simpson's U.S. Ninth Army, and Hodges' V, VII and XVIII (Airborne) Corps, would fall under Montgomery. Patton's Third Army, now including what was left of Middleton's VIII Corps, would remain under Bradley. The changeover would take effect from 1200 hrs next day, 20 December.

If Montgomery was elated, Bradley was aghast. If it had been anyone other than Montgomery, he could have accepted the decision. But this left him fuming. Hodges was also unhappy, and when Montgomery arrived at his headquarters, one of his officers was to remark that it was like 'Christ come to cleanse the Temple'. Montgomery's attitude was supercilious and reflected his belief that, if he *had* earlier been given total command on the ground, the Americans would

not have got themselves into this mess. It was not an attitude which endeared him to many people in the United States, but worse was to come when he later claimed the victory as a British one – a rash statement to the press which almost got him sacked and which forced Prime Minister Winston Churchill to apologise in the House of Commons.

But that lay in the future as Montgomery studied the situation map in Hodges' headquarters. He immediately proposed withdrawing from St Vith to straighten the line and moving Major-General Lawton 'Lightning Joe' Collins' VII Corps south to follow its 3rd Armored Division and create a strong reserve behind the River Ourthe. He also took 2nd Armored Division away from Ninth Army and sent it in the same direction, and began moving British reserves from XXX Corps to

U.S. PARACHUTE INFANTRY COMPANY
(116 men)

Officers: 1 Captain, 1 Lieutenant (each 1 x .45 Colt automatic & 1 x .45 Thompson M1/M1A1 or .45 M3/M3A1 SMG)
NCOs: 1 Technical Sergeant, 4 Platoon Sergeants (each 1 x .45 Thompson M1/M1A1 or .45 M3/M3A1 SMG)
Weapons Platoon (Lieutenant and/or Sergeant) 27 men, 1 x 81m mortar, 3 x 60mm mortar, 3 x .30 M1918A2 Browning Automatic Rifle (BAR), 24 x .30 M1A1/M2 carbine
1st Rifle Platoon (Sergeant)
  Squad 1 (9 men) 1 x bazooka, 1 x BAR,
   7 x M1A1/M2 carbine
  Squad 2 As above
  Squad 3 As above
2nd Rifle Platoon (Three squads as above)
3rd Rifle Platoon (Three squads as above)

Notes:
1. Because the Thompson was always in short supply and the M3 'grease gun', a utility weapon like the British Sten, was not highly regarded, many veterans carried captured German MP38s or MP40s.
2. The BAR can be classed as either a heavy assault rifle or a light machine-gun but, when fitted with a bipod, was usually used in the latter role.
3. The M1 carbine was originally introduced to supplement the M1 Garand rifle as a secondary weapon for mortar and machine-gun crews, but was widely used by the airborne forces because of its small size and light weight.
The M1A1 had a folding stock and the M2 a full automatic fire capability.

block the natural crossing points over the Meuse between Dinant and Liège.

Montgomery was essentially a defensive player; solicitous of his men to be sure but, in that conservatism, unwilling to take risks. This was the way he had won at El Alamein, and the only time he had thrown away his normal *modus operandi*, for 'Market Garden', the operation had been a disaster. So, when he summoned Bradley to his headquarters in Zonhoven, Holland, on Christmas Day (not even offering him lunch), he appeared timorous to his American opposite number. Bradley, along with Hodges and Patton, wanted to counter-attack immediately. (Neither of them knew that, at this precise moment, 2nd Armored Division was giving 2 Panzer Division a bloody nose at Celles, just east of Dinant, which would mark the high tide line of the German advance.) Montgomery, however, insisted that the Germans still had something up their sleeve, and that the Americans should not only remain on the defensive but even fall back further to allow time for more reserves to be built up. His opinion was, in fact, ratified by the British Joint Intelligence Committee whose members believed that the Germans 'might well release additional reserves for a final lunge'.

That did not fit in with what Eisenhower, placing

Men of C Company, 23rd Armored Infantry Battalion, advance to reinforce the defenders at Prümerberg during late afternoon on 17 December. (U.S. Army)

U.S. 'LIGHT' ARMORED DIVISION
(c. 12,000 men)
Division HQ & HQ Company
(3 x M5 Stuart or M24 Chaffee, 16 x M3 half-track, 3 x 57mm M1, 8 x .50 HMG, 10 x .30 LMG & 14 x bazooka)
(c. 300 men)

COMBAT COMMAND A
HQ Company (c. 70 men)
(3 x M5 or M24, 7 x M3, 4 x .50 HMG, 3 x .30 LMG &
8 x bazooka)

COMBAT COMMAND B
(as above)

COMBAT COMMAND R
(as above)

TANK BATTALION (x 3) (c. 740 men)
HQ Company (2 x M4 [75mm])
A, B & C Companies (each 17 x M4 [75mm] &
2 x M4 [105mm])
D Company (17 x M5 or M24)

ARMORED INFANTRY BATTALION (x 3) (c. 1,000 men)
HQ Company (1 x 81mm mortar, 1 x .50 HMG, 1 x .30 HMG,
2 x .30 LMG & 2 x bazooka)
A, B & C Companies (each 1 x 75mm M3 GMC,
1 x 81mm mortar M3, 24 x M3, 3 x 57mm M1,
3 x 60mm mortar, 14 x .50 HMG, 12 x .30 HMG,
7 x .30 LMG & 24 x bazooka)

ARMORED FIELD ARTILLERY BATTALION (x 3) (c. 540 men)
HQ Company (2 x M3 half-track)
A, B & C Batteries (each 6 x 105mm M7 GMC & 10 x M3)

CAVALRY RECONNAISSANCE SQUADRON, MECHANIZED
(c. 930 men)
HQ Troop (1 x M8, 2 x M3, 2 x .50 HMG & 2 x bazooka)
A, B & C Troops (each 17 x M8, 10 x M3, 1 x 81mm mortar,
12 x 60mm mortar, 9 x .50 HMG, 20 x .30 LMG &
10 x bazooka)

Light Tank Troop (17 x M5/M24)
Support Troop (8 x 75mm M3 GMC, 8 x .30 LMG &
5 x bazooka)

ANTI-AIRCRAFT ARTILLERY AUTO-WEAPONS BATTALION
(c. 720 men) (attached one per division)
HQ Company
A, B, C & D Companies (each 8 x M16); Note – 90mm M1A1
towed AA guns also sometimes attached

TANK DESTROYER BATTALION (c. 700 men) (attached)
As per Infantry Division

DIVISION TRAINS (c. 100 men)
HQ & HQ Company

MEDICAL BATTALION, ARMORED (c. 415 men)
HQ Company
A & B Companies (each 2 x M3 ambulance & 3 x surgical truck)

ARMORED ORDNANCE MAINTENANCE BATTALION
(c. 760 men)
HQ Company (1 x M3, 8 x .50 HMG, 4 x .30 LMG & 5 bazooka)
A, B & C Companies (each 1 x M3, 10 x .50 HMG,
8 x .30 LMG & 10 bazooka)

MILITARY POLICE PLATOON (c. 90 men)

ARMORED ENGINEER BATTALION (c. 690 men)
HQ Company (2 x M3, 2 x .50 HMG & 2 x bazooka)
A, B & C Companies (each 5 x M3, 6 x .50 HMG,
6 x .30 LMG & 9 x bazooka)

ARMORED SIGNAL COMPANY (c. 300 men)
(19 x M3, 13 x .50 HMG, 13 x .30 LMG & 24 x bazooka)

more reliance on 'Ultra' transcripts, believed. These clearly showed that the Germans were at the end of their tether, having suffered heavy tank losses and being unable to keep their spearheads supplied, particularly with fuel. He, like Bradley, wanted Montgomery to attack, but when the two men met in Bruxelles on 28 December, he had to go away content with Montgomery's promise that if a new German threat had not materialised, he would begin his own attack on 3 January. Then Montgomery overplayed his hand. He wrote to Eisenhower the following day dictating a directive giving him 'full operational direction, control and coordination' of 'all available offensive power'. This was the last straw. Eisehower offered to resign and both Bradley and Patton said they would not serve under Montgomery.

The Field Marshal was forced to apologise to save his own career and Eisenhower directed Hodges and Patton to begin driving their armies together to pinch off the 'bulge'.

Below left: The crew of an 81mm mortar dug-in just outside St Vith. Mortars were invaluable in breaking up infantry attacks. (U.S. Army)
Below: Lines of communication in defence (interior lines). This map uses 7th Armored Division's three combat commands with HQ in St Vith as an example. All commands were linked by radio which proved unreliable so physical communication was preferred where possible. Bad weather and the state of the roads militated against dispatch riders so it is no wonder that messages and orders were often delayed.

Overleaf, pages 16–17: What did the Allies know? Their expectations mirrored one of Model's early ideas, which was rejected by Hitler, but later incorporated again as part of the 'small solution'. The Allies have an enclave around Aachen but are threatened by salients north at Roermond and south at Monschau (not shown). All enemy troop movements were interpreted as leading towards a German pincer attack, a misbelief the Germans did all they could to encourage. This, coupled with a lack of aerial reconnaissance because of bad weather, added to Allied confusion when the Germans launched Operation 'Herbstnebel'.

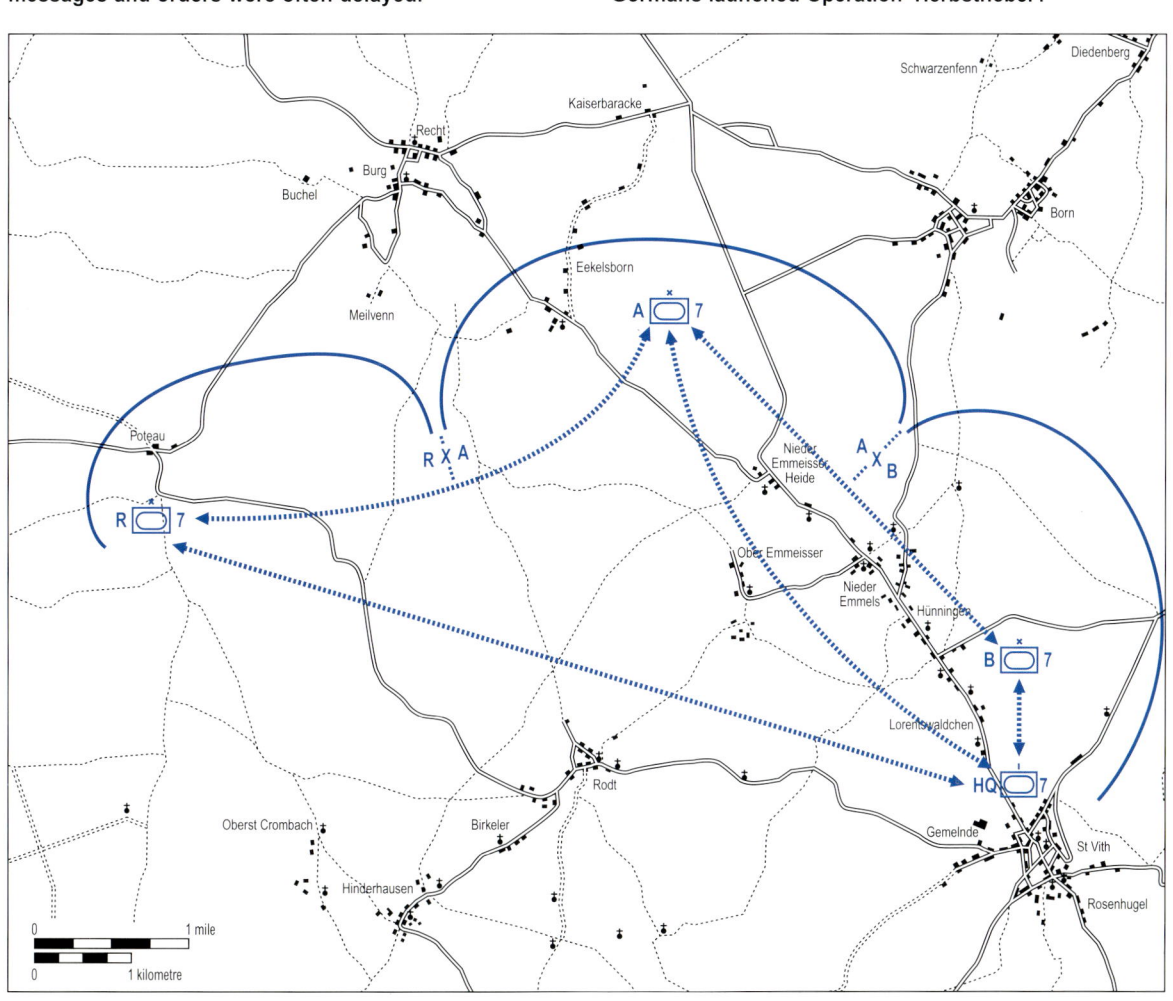

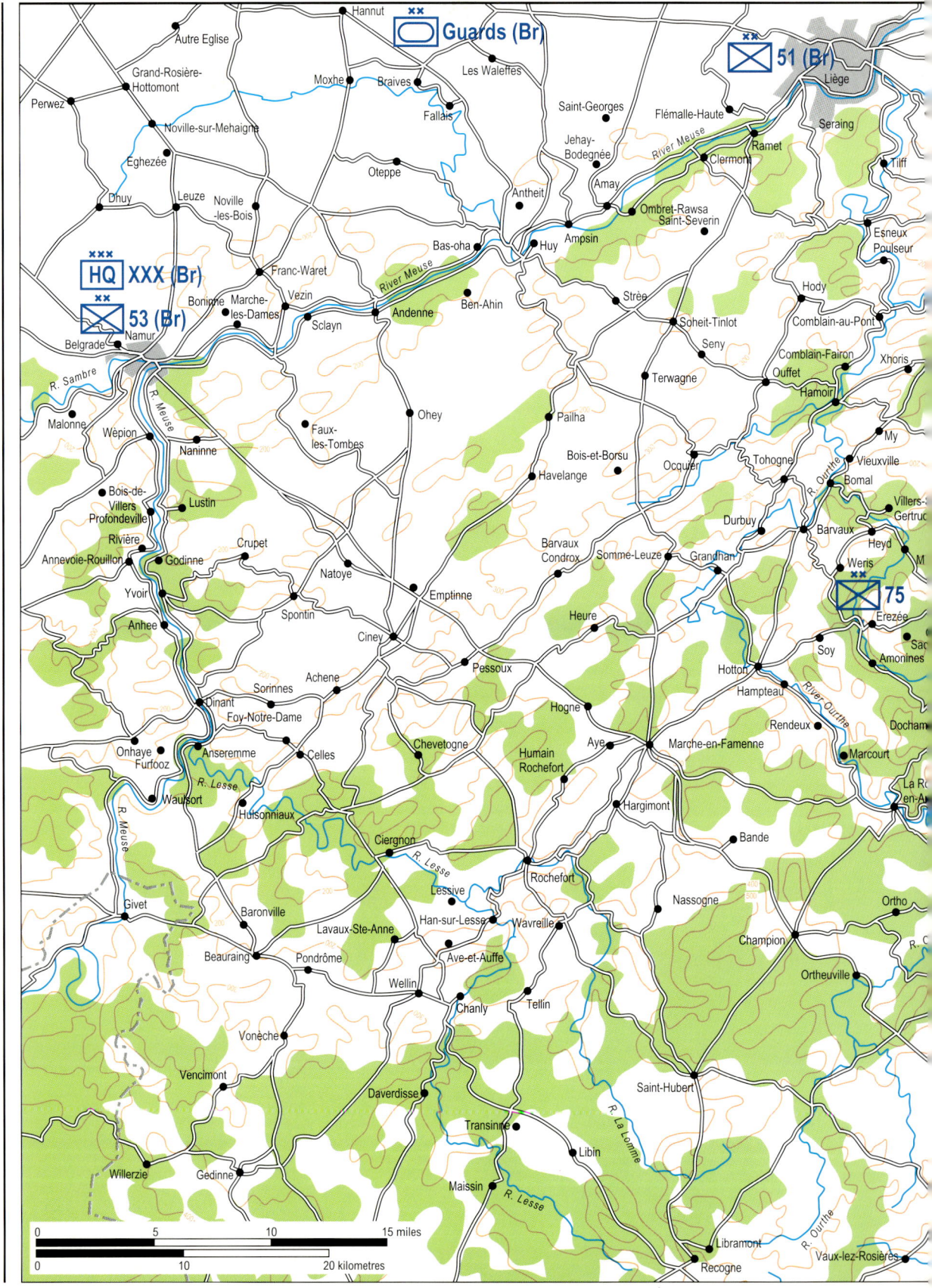

Hannut

Guards (Br)

51 (Br)

Autre Eglise

Grand-Rosière-Hottomont

Moxhe

Braives

Les Waleffes

Liège

Perwez

Fallais

Saint-Georges

Flémalle-Haute

Seraing

Noville-sur-Mehaigne

Jehay-Bodegnée

Amay

Ombret-Rawsa
Saint-Severin

Ramet

Clermont

Tilff

Eghezée

Oteppe

Antheit

Dhuy

Leuze

Noville
-les-Bois

Bas-oha

Huy

Ampsin

Esneux
Poulseur

HQ XXX (Br)

Franc-Waret

Vezin

River Meuse

River Meuse

Strée

Soheit-Tinlot

Seny

Hody

Comblain-au-Pont

53 (Br)

Bonique

Marche-
les-Dames

Belgrade

Namur

Sclayn

Andenne

Ben-Ahin

Comblain-Fairon

Ouffet

Xhoris

Hamoir

Terwagne

R. Sambre

Malonne

Wépion

Ohey

Pailha

Tohogne

My

Vieuxville

R. Meuse

Naninne

Faux-
les-Tombes

Bois-et-Borsu

Havelange

Ocquier

R. Ourthe

Bomal

Villers-:
Gertruc

Bois-de-
Villers
Profondeville

Lustin

Durbuy

Barvaux

Heyd

M

Rivière

Crupet

Barvaux
Condrox

Somme-Leuze

Grandhan

Weris

Annevoie-Rouillon

Godinne

Natoye

Emptinne

Heure

75

Erezée

Yvoir

Spontin

Ciney

Soy

Sac

Anhée

Amonines

Achene

Pessoux

Hotton

Sorrinnes

Hogne

Hampteau

River Ourthe

Dinant

Foy-Notre-Dame

Aye

Marche-en-Famenne

Rendeux

Docham

Onhaye
Furfooz

Anseremme

Celles

Chevetogne

Humain
Rochefort

Marcourt

La R
en-A

Waulsort

R. Lesse

Hargimont

Huisonniaux

Ciergnon

Bande

R. Lesse

Rochefort

Givet

Baronville

Lessive

Nassogne

Ortho

R. C

Lavaux-Ste-Anne

Han-sur-Lesse

Wavreille

Champion

Beauraing

Pondrôme

Ave-et-Auffe

Ortheuville

R. Meuse

Wellin

Chanly

Tellin

Vonèche

Saint-Hubert

Vencimont

Daverdisse

R. La Lomme

Transinne

Willerzie

Gedinne

Libin

R. Ourthe

Maissin

R. Lesse

Libramont

Vaux-lez-Rosières

Recogne

0   5   10   15 miles

0   10   20 kilometres

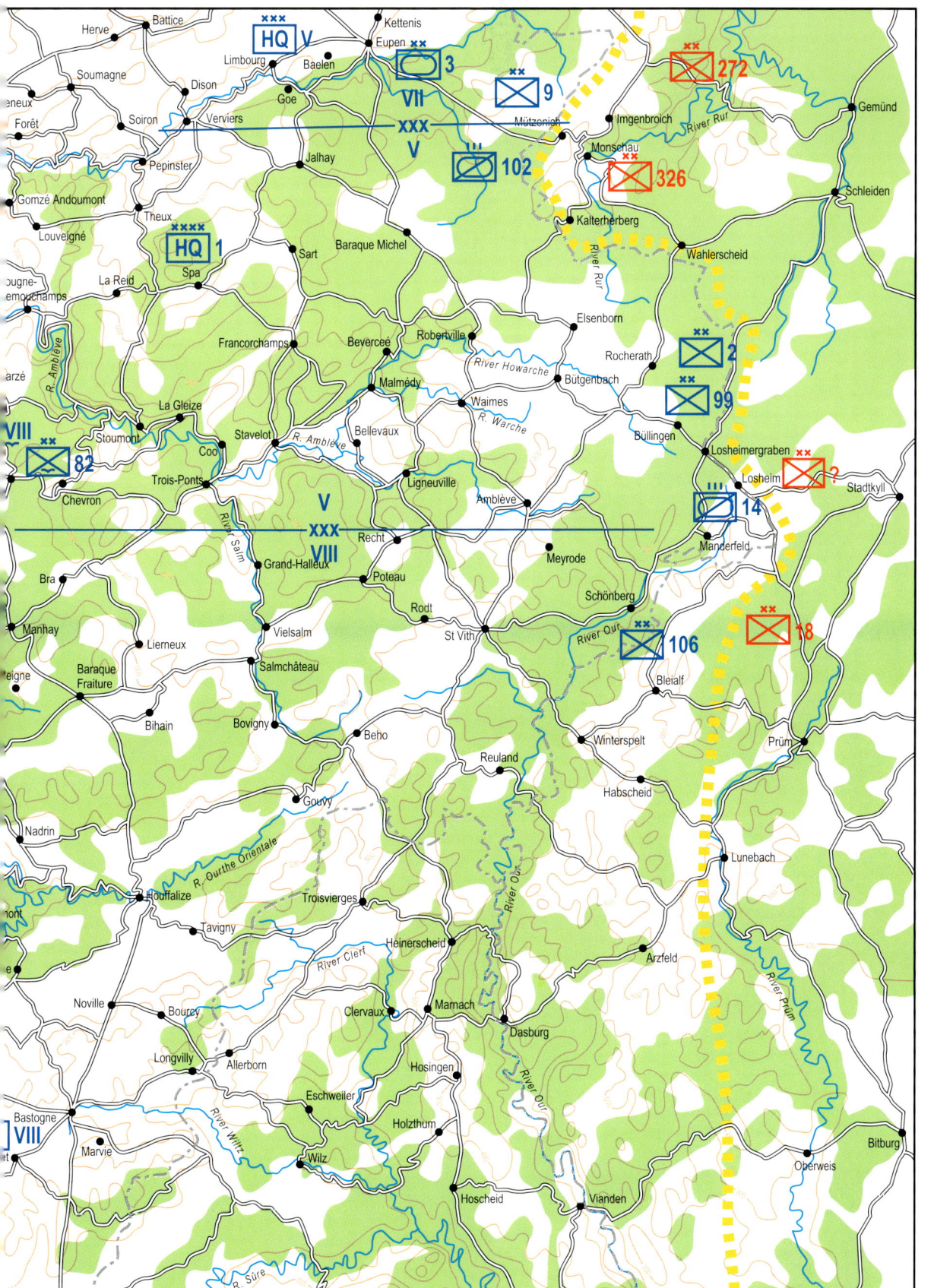

U.S. FIRST ARMY

irst Army commander Courtney Hicks Hodges was rarely known to smile and his normal expression was, to say the least, lugubrious. On the morning of 20 December 1944, however, he had a valid reason to look glum. It was not that his men were failing to hold against the pride of the Wehrmacht and Waffen-SS in the biggest German counter-attack since Normandy in the summer, albeit in places by the skin of their teeth. Neither was it that he was short of reinforcements, because some had already arrived and more were on their way. Nor was he short of fuel or ammunition. Moreover, he had implicit faith in the competence of his V and VII Corps' commanders, Leonard Gerow and Joseph Collins; and although he really only knew Matthew Ridgway by reputation, he

U.S. FIRST ARMY
Lieutenant-General Courtney H. Hodges
Chief of Staff:
Major-General William G. Kean

V CORPS (Gerow)
VII CORPS (Collins)
VIII CORPS (Middleton)
XVIII (AIRBORNE) CORPS (Gavin pp. Ridgway)
 (attached from SHAEF Reserve)
5 Fusilier Battalion (Belgian)
99 Infantry Battalion (The Norwegians)
526 Armored Infantry Battalion
143 Anti-Aircraft Artillery Gun Battalion (Mobile)
413 Anti-Aircraft Artillery Gun Battalion (Mobile)

Lieutenant-General Courtney Hicks Hodges had been Bradley's deputy before the latter was given overall command of First, Third and Ninth Armies.
(U.S. Signal Corps)

was certain that XVIII (Airborne) Corps would not let him down either.

What really griped Hodges, this morning of 20 December, four days into the German offensive, was that from now on he would have to take orders from that 'pipsqueak', Montgomery, instead of the superior officer he knew intimately and trusted, Omar Bradley. If Hodges had known that the change in command had been Montgomery's own suggestion, and that Eisen-hower had assented, he would certainly have been even more discomfitted. As it was, the Field

Marshal's casual lack of courtesy when he visited Hodges' new headquarters in Chaudfontaine still served to fuel the resentment because, not only had 'Monty' brought his own situation map with him, but a lunchbox and thermos flask as well!

Hodges' attitude is perfectly understandable, even though Montgomery's habits were always this ascetic, and he eschewed ceremony. Ironically, the two men had much in common. They were the same age, both born in 1887, and had both been decorated in World War 1, Montgomery with the Distinguished Service Order and Hodges with the Distinguished Service Cross. One difference was that the studious Montgomery had excelled at Sandhurst whereas Hodges had been forced to leave West Point because he failed his geometry exam. Hodges had promptly re-enlisted as a Private but was commissioned 2nd Lieutenant only a year later and served under Brigadier-General John Pershing (as did Patton) in the Mexican expedition of 1916-17 against Pancho Villa before commanding a machine-gun company on the Western Front in 1918.

Welcome reinforcements for First Army: men of the 291st Regiment, 75th Infantry Division, with an M4 Sherman, advance towards the front.
(U.S. Signal Corps)

In the interwar years both men followed a similar path through staff and individual command posts, and after their countries' entry into the war in 1939 and 1941 respectively, both were soon given Corps to command, Montgomery the British V and Hodges the U.S. X. In 1942 Montgomery was appointed to lead the British Eighth Army in North Africa, and six months later Hodges the U.S. Third in Italy. Thereafter, though, as a result of his victory at El Alamein, Montgomery's star ascended faster, and from D-Day until the end of August 1944 he commanded all Allied ground forces in France, American, British and Canadian, while Hodges was serving as Bradley's deputy in the U.S. First Army.

When Eisenhower himself took over Montgomery's role on 1 September, diplomatically pouring oil over the increasing rift between Bradley and Montgomery and leaving the Field Marshal with 'just' the 21st Army Group to command, Montgomery felt slighted and his resentment became an increasing canker in SHAEF. Hodges, on the other hand, was delighted to be given the U.S. First Army as his own following Bradley's appointment to command the 12th Army Group. Now, however, Hodges was being forced to serve under

Montgomery again, and he did not like it. Fortunately, he was thoroughly professional enough not to allow the changeover to affect his decision-taking ability, although it did chafe that Montgomery was so slow in resuming an offensive stance.

By Christmas, or at least 26 December, it was clear to everyone from Eisenhower down – except to Montgomery – that the German offensive had run out of steam. They were making, and would continue to make, increasingly desperate attempts to rupture the Bastogne corridor, but the emergency was over as far as First Army was concerned. I SS-Panzer Korps had been well and truly stopped, and II SS-Panzer Korps now stood no chance of breaking through at Erezée, so now was the time to change the roles of hunter and prey. But Montgomery still objected, insisting that the Germans had more aces to play, and remained on the defensive until he had built up what he considered sufficient reserves. Fortunately for Hodges' powers of restraint, this situation did not last long.

Eisenhower had stressed to the Field Marshal that his appointment to command all Allied forces north of 'the bulge' was only a temporary expedient. That Montgomery chose to interpret it differently is a measure of his egocentricity. However, he was very promptly disabused.

On 30 December, ten days after Montgomery's appointment and a day after his letter to Eisenhower demanding 'full operational direction, control and

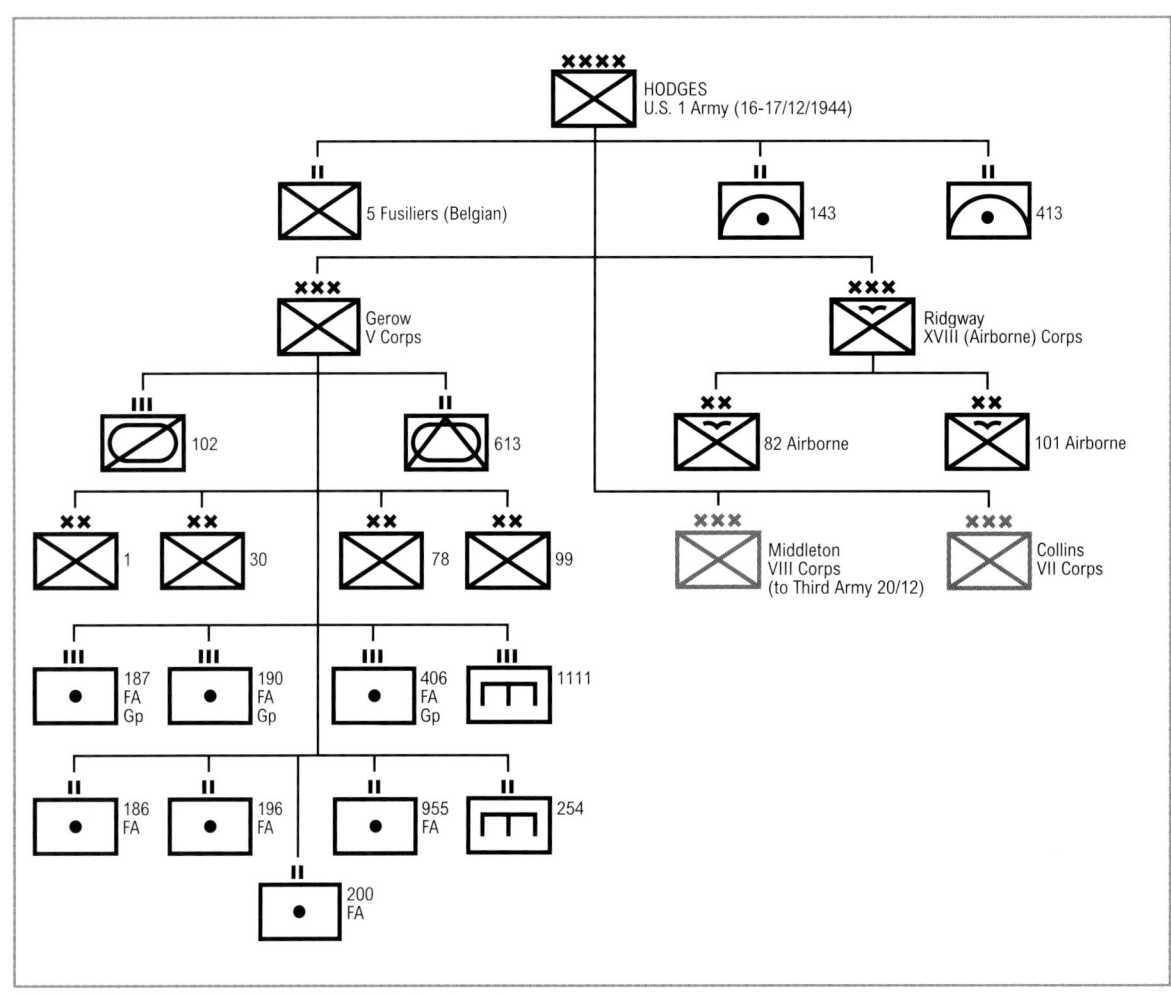

co-ordination' of 'all offensive power', a liaison officer at SHAEF headquarters in Versailles leaked news of Eisenhower's anger to Montgomery's chief of staff, Major-General Francis de Guingand. 'Freddie' flew to Paris the moment the weather permitted and found Eisenhower in the small house in Versailles where he had been forced to live since a rumour started that Otto Skorzeny's 'Greif' commandos were out to assassinate him.

By this time Eisenhower had drafted a letter to go to the Combined Chiefs of Staff stating bluntly that they would have to choose between Montgomery and himself. Given the fact that there were far more United States' troops on the continent than British, Eisen-hower was in a secure position. Even so, he acceded to de Guingand's plea to withhold the letter for a day, and 'Freddie' flew back to Holland to see Montgomery immediately. The Field Marshal was shattered by de Guingand's news – his chief of staff said later that he had never seen him 'so deflated' – and immediately wrote a second letter to Eisenhower

promising his wholehearted support and urging the Supreme Commander to tear up the earlier letter. 'Ike' relented, but told Montgomery that the U.S. First Army would revert to Bradley's 12th Army Group the moment it had established contact with the troops of Patton's Third Army.

The Allied plan to erase the 'bulge' finally adopted had been proposed by Hodges' VII Corps' commander, Joseph Collins. It was less ambitious than that suggested by Patton, and aimed only at cutting off those German forces roughly west of a line Bastogne-Houffalize-St Vith rather than further east. VII Corps was to administer the punch towards Houffalize to link up with Troy Middleton's VIII Corps north of Bastogne; meanwhile, Major-General Manton Eddy's XII Corps was to drive north from west of Echternach, and Major-General John Millikin's III Corps was to strike east from south of Bastogne, while the four divisions of First Army's XVIII (Airborne) Corps – 7th Armored, 30th and 75th Infantry and 82nd Airborne – pushed back east towards St Vith, straightening the line with

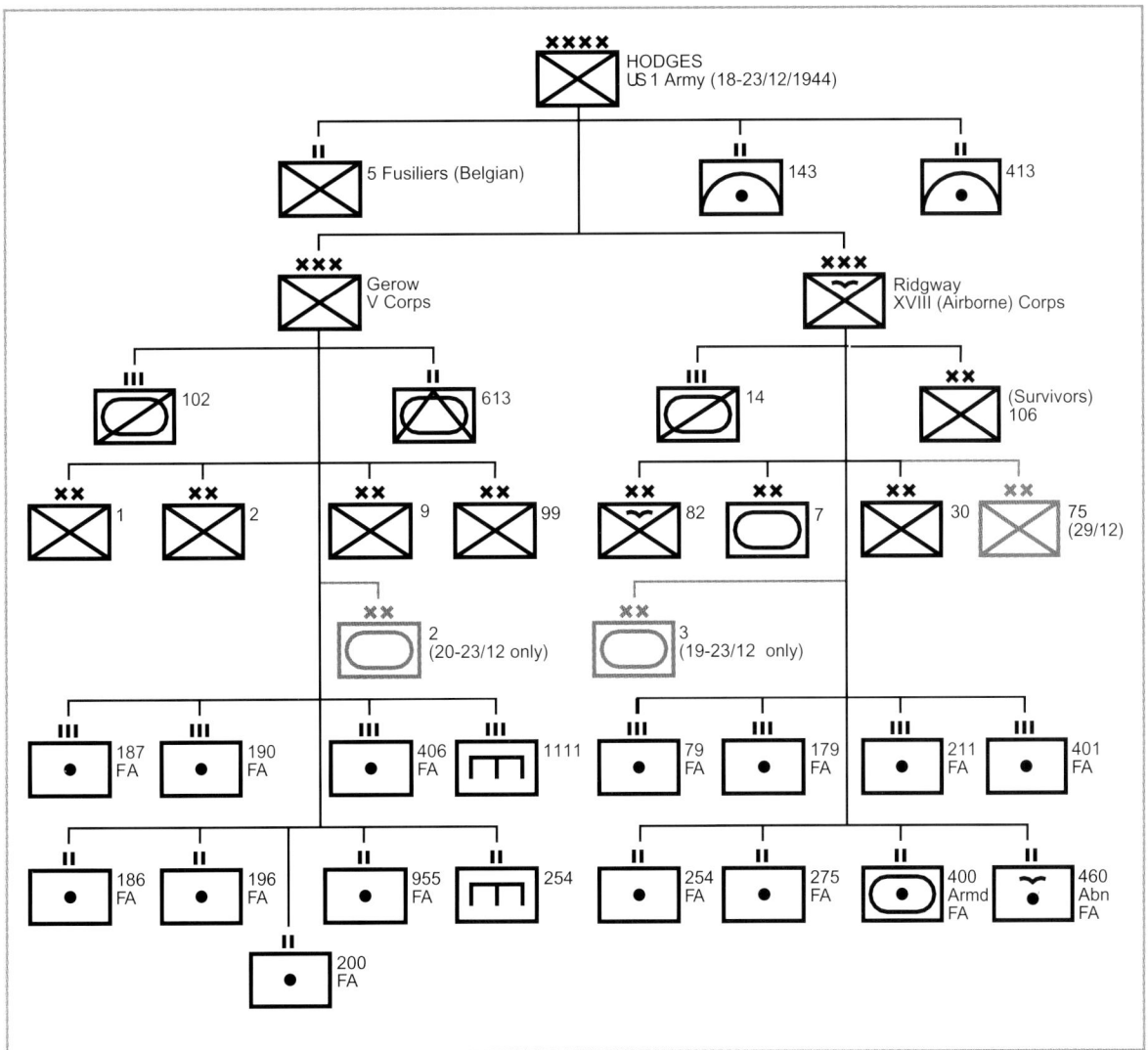

V Corps in the north. First Army's role was, in fact, the crucial one, because Patton's forces in the south were under increasing pressure as Feldmarschall Walter Model moved more and more divisions into the Bastogne sector.

The counter-offensive began on 3 January 1945; within 24 hours there was no longer any threat to Bastogne; four days later Hitler authorised Model to begin a limited withdrawal; and on the 16th patrols from Collins' 84th Infantry and Middleton's 11th Armored Divisions met outside Houffalize. Next day, First Army reverted to Omar Bradley's command, but the rift in Anglo-American relations stirred up by Montgomery and the British press was not soothed until Winston Churchill told the House of Commons on the 18th that the battle in the Ardennes was 'the greatest American battle of the war and will be regarded as an ever famous American victory'.

By this generous, even if belated concession, Churchill was acknowledging that the real victory belonged to Bradley, Hodges and Patton and not to Montgomery, even though the Field Marshal's apologists insist to this day that it was his firm control over the northern sector of the front from 20 December which saved the Americans' bacon. But in truth the real victory belonged, not to the commanders, but to the ordinary men of First and Third Armies and, while Patton's drive to relieve Bastogne grabbed most of the headlines, it was the dogged determination of Hodges' troops on Elsenborn ridge and at St Vith which had stopped the strongest of the three German armies deployed in the offensive, Sixth Panzer.

'Sepp' Dietrich, the Sixth Panzer Armee commander, would dearly have loved to have had First Army to command for his part in the offensive. One enormous advantage Hodges enjoyed was mobility. In Dietrich's

Volksgrenadier divisions, everyone walked; in Hodges', the infantry rode in trucks up to their assembly areas. A typical U.S. infantry division had over 1,300 trucks from quarter-tonners to four-tonners, Only in the German Panzergrenadier regiments were the infantry motorised, one battalion in armoured half-tracks, the second in trucks. In Hodges' army, the three armoured infantry battalions in an armoured division had 150 M3 half-tracks each. What vehicles Dietrich did have were constantly immobilised for lack of fuel; in Hodges' V Corps' area alone, the three huge POL depots outside Büllingen, Stavelot and La Gleize would have kept I SS-Panzer Korps running for a week.

It was not, therefore, just mobility that Hodges' First Army enjoyed; it was enormous matériel superiority. German artillery support for attacks was often weak because the gunners had only limited ammunition; Hodges' gunners could afford to be profligate, and time after time during the containment phase of the 'battle of the bulge' it was the artillery which broke up the German attacks, creating killing fields in which nothing could survive.

If the quality of the average U.S. infantryman during World War 2 has often been called into question, not so the artillery, which was greatly admired by the Germans. Each infantry division had four field artillery battalions with 36 105mm and 12 155mm howitzers between them – and all drawn by trucks or tractors whereas the field artillery in Dietrich's Volksgrenadier divisions was almost entirely horse-drawn. Only in the Panzer divisions was it motorised. Nor were Hodges' gunners ill-trained, unlike some of his infantry in the higher-numbered divisions; to an artilleryman, a battlefield is often little different from a training exercise, apart from the risk of genuine rather than simulated counter-battery fire. In the Ardennes, this was rarely encountered, because the Germans had to conserve their ammunition for softening up the American infantry positions. Moreover, the U.S. Army gunners had the advantage of the hitherto top secret POZIT proximity fuze, which caused their shells to burst overhead of the attacking German infantry battalions, causing consternation and an understandable degree of panic along with very heavy casualties.

Only in their armoured and Panzer divisions did Hodges and Dietrich have anything like artillery parity, because both utilised armoured self-propelled guns, the Germans the 105mm 'Wespe' and 155mm 'Hummel', the Americans the 105mm M7 GMC 'Priest' of which there were 36 organic to an armoured field artillery regiment; the 155mm M40 GMC 'Long Toms' were deployed in battalions of 12 at corps level.

In anti-tank artillery, however, Dietrich did have an advantage over Hodges. The standard American infantry anti-tank gun issued on a scale of six per battalion was the little 57mm M1, a longer-barrelled version of the British six-pounder. By this stage of the war this weapon was of little more than nuisance value; except by a lucky shot at close range, it was incapable of doing more damage to a Panther or Tiger than breaking a track. (Fortunately, Dietrich had only a handful of Tigers even though, reading some combat accounts, you would have thought the Ardennes were swarming with them.) By contrast to the M1, the Germans had the excellent 75mm PaK 40 which could easily knock out a Sherman; and the 88mm PaK 43. In self-propelled anti-tank guns the story was similar. Hodges' tank destroyer battalions had a preponderance of M10s and M18s with 3-inch (76mm) guns and a few M36s with 90mm weapons. They had the advantage over German jagdpanzers of fully-traversing turrets, but these were open-topped, making their crews vulnerable to high explosive artillery and mortar fire. They were also more lightly armoured (particularly the M18) than the German Jagdpanzer IV/70s and Jagdpanthers, and neither the American 76mm nor the 90mm gun was a match for the longer-barrelled German 75mm and 88mm weapons, whose higher muzzle velocity, except at close quarters, conferred an enormous advantage. Where, however, Hodges' weaponry may have been inferior to Dietrich's, he had much more of it, and counter-attacks by V, VII and XVIII Corps tank destroyer battalions were often highly effective even though they often suffered through being deployed piecemeal rather than decisively en masse.

The same story applies to American and German tanks. The U.S. Army had standardised the M4 Sherman (albeit in a number of different variants) since 1942. While this had a good turn of speed, it was insufficiently protected against late-war anti-tank projectiles, and its relatively short-barrelled 75/76mm gun was outclassed by the same calibre weapons in later marks of the PzKpfw IV, let alone those in the Panther or Tiger. Again, American superiority lay in quantity rather than quality, but it needed good leadership to function effectively, and when this was missing as it had sometimes been in Normandy and during the pursuit across France – First Army's armoured formations were at a distinct disadvantage compared with their highly-experienced German counterparts.

Prior to D-Day, the Allies had studied the German use of kampfgruppen – battlegroups – to give them operational flexibility. The U.S. Army had tried to emulate this by breaking its armoured divisions down

The 155mm 'Long Tom' equipped the U.S. Army's medium artillery battalions, while the field artillery was armed with 105mm pieces. Both played a decisive role in the Ardennes. (U.S. Signal Corps)

into three Combat Commands (four in the 'heavy' 2nd and 3rd Armored Divisions), CCA, CCB and CCR (Reserve). Although CCR was so labelled, in fact the commands were interchangeable. Each was a balanced battlegroup combining tanks, tank destroyers, armoured infantry and self-propelled artillery. However, having sought flexibility, the Army had actually created a quite rigid structure, whereas the composition of a German kampfgruppe was usually tailor-made for a specific operation. Nevertheless, in the hands of a good commander, such as Robert Hasbrouck of 7th or Maurice Rose of 3rd Armored Division, the Combat Command system could be made to work very effectively, as during the battle for St Vith and the counter-attacks in the Amblève valley around Stoumont, La Gleize and Stavelot.

If there was a weakness in the U.S. Army as a whole, it did lie in the infantry. This was a result of the selective system employed, in which any draftee with higher educational qualifications, or proven mechanical or electrical skills, was automatically posted to one of the technical branches. This left the infantry – except

in the élite airborne regiments – largely uneducated and sometimes difficult to train or motivate. In the veteran divisions, such as the 1st which had fought its way through North Africa and Sicily before coming ashore on D-Day, the situation was not so bad. They took pride in their achievements and this was rapidly communicated to the replacements in their ranks (the U.S. Army terminology was 'reinforcements' for better psychological effect on the newcomers). In the newer divisions, this was not the case because, although they benefited from improved training based upon European combat experience, their ranks were constantly being drained to replace casualties in the existing divisions. Thus, the men of Hodges' 99th Infantry Division, for example, which had only just arrived in Europe, were largely untrained, despite the apparent length of the division's training programme.

In broad terms, the new 'reinforcements' performed admirably in the Ardennes, particularly when on the defence and with good leadership at junior levels (lieutenant and captain). In the attack, they were less certain and suffered from limited firepower, lacking anything resembling the German assault rifle at this time. The result was uneven performance, but at the end of the day Hodges could, overall, be as proud of the First Army 'greenhorns' as he was of the veterans. They had, after all, given the enemy a bloody nose.

U.S. FIRST ARMY

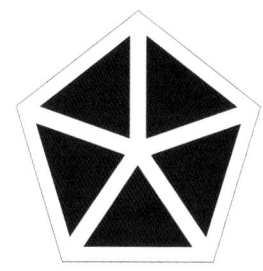

U.S. V CORPS

The deployment of Major-General Leonard T. Gerow's V Corps in the last few days leading up to the 'battle of the bulge' had a decisive effect on its outcome even though two of his infantry divisions were only peripherally involved and he had to circumvent a direct order from Courtney Hodges in order to salvage the situation on 16-17 December.

With major offensives imminent towards both the Ruhr and Saar industrial regions of Germany north and south of the 'quiet' Eupen/Monschau sector, there

Major-General Leonard T. Gerow disobeyed orders on 16 December but his prompt action saved Elsenborn ridge from being overrun.
(U.S. Signal Corps)

was still a thorn in the centre of the Allied front line in December 1944. This was the threat posed by the millions of gallons of water in the reservoirs backed up behind the Schwammenauel and Urftalsperre dams fed by the rivers Rur and Urft to the east of Monschau. A major First Army attack in this sector with the undamaged dams still in German hands could have resulted in the troops being submerged in a veritable tidal wave of mud and water. Efforts by Allied air forces 'dambuster' bombers to breach the dams at the beginning of December had been ineffectual so on 7 Dec-ember, following a SHAEF conference presided over by Eisenhower at Maastricht, Bradley ordered Hodges to use his centre corps, which at this time was Gerow's V Corps, to seize them.

Some commanders might have objected to putting their men into deliberate jeopardy in this fashion,

but by this stage of the war, Bradley and Hodges had come to trust the testy, outspoken and somewhat impetuous Gerow, even though he had nearly caused a diplomatic rupture with the French earlier in the year. It he had led his men all the way once they got off 'Omaha' beach with consummate skill. Prior to D-Day, Gerow had not commanded a fighting formation, although he had been CO of the 29th Infantry Division at Fort Meade, Maryland, for six months in 1942.

V CORPS
Major-General Leonard T. Gerow
Deputy and Chief of Staff:
Major-General Clarence R. Huebner

---

1 Infantry Division (Andrus)
2 Infantry Division (Robertson)
  (from VIII Corps 20 December)
9 Infantry Division (Cralg)
  (from VII Corps 18 December)
30 Infantry Division (Hobbs)
  (to XVIII Corps 21 December)
78 Infantry Division (Parker)
  (to VII Corps 18 December)
99 Infantry Division (Lauer)
102 Cavalry Group (Mechanized):
  38 & 102 Cavalry Squadrons (Mechanized)
612 Tank Destroyer Battalion
187 Field Artillery Group:
  751 and 997 Field Artillery Battalions
190 Field Artillery Group: 62, 190, 268 & 272 Field Artillery Battalions
406 Field Artillery Group: 76, 941, 953 & 987 Field Artillery Battalions
186 Field Artillery Battalion
196 Field Artillery Battalion
200 Field Artillery Battalion
955 Field Artillery Battalion
1111 Engineer Combat Group (Anderson):
  51, 202, 291 and 296 Engineer Combat Battalions
254 Engineer Combat Battalion
(2 Armored Division [Harmon]
  [briefly attached 20-23 December en route to VII Corps])

US V CORPS TROOPS

102 Cavalry Group (c. 1,500 men)
Group HQ & HQ Troop

38 & 102 Cavalry Reconnaissance Squadrons, Mechanized
HQ Troop (4 x M8, 2 x M3, 1 x .50 HMG & 1 x bazooka)
A, B & C Troops
(each 12 x M8, 8 x M3, 1 x 81mm mortar, 9 x 60mm
mortar, 8 x .50 HMG, 18 x .30 LMG & 10 x bazooka)
Light Tank Troop (17 x M5/M24)
Support Troop (6 x 75mm M3 GMC)

187 Field Artillery Group

751 Field Artillery Battalion (12 x 155mm M1A1 howitzer,
tractor-drawn)
997 Field Artillery Battalion (6 x 8" M1 howitzer,
tractor-drawn)

190 Field Artillery Group

62 Field Artillery Battalion (12 x 105mm M2A1 howitzer,
truck-drawn)
190 Field Artillery Battalion (12 x 155mm M1 gun,
tractor-drawn)
268 Field Artillery Battalion (6 x 8" M1 howitzer,
tractor-drawn)
272 Field Artillery Battalion (12 x 240mm M1 howitzer,
truck-drawn)

406 Field Artillery Group

76 Field Artillery Battalion (12 x 105mm M2A1 howitzer,
truck-drawn)
941 Field Artillery Battalion (12 x 4.5" M1 gun, tractor-drawn)
953 Field Artillery Battalion (12 x 155mm M1A1 howitzer,
tractor-drawn)
987 Field Artillery Battalion (12 x 155mm M12 GMC)

Field Artillery Battalions

186 (12 x 155mm M1A1 howitzer, tractor-drawn)
196 (12 x 105mm M2A1 howitzer, truck-drawn)
200 (12 x 155mm M1 gun, tractor-drawn)
955 (12 x 155mm M1A1 howitzer, tractor-drawn)

His performance compared with some of Bradley's other more experienced commanders such as Collins and Middleton was, thus, all the more creditable.

V Corps had been chosen for the left prong of First Army's assault on D-Day across 'Omaha' beach which, as it turned out, was the most heavily and skilfully defended. Gerow relied on his infantry to carry the day and did not accept the offer of some of the British 79th Armoured Division's specialised 'funnies' which, alongside inexperience, contributed to his severe losses; he may have been influenced by the fact that his former 116th Regiment from the 29th Infantry Division was attached to the veteran 1st Infantry Division in the first wave of the assault, and wanted to prove that it was just as good as they were.

Unfortunately, unnerved by the heavy and accurate German fire after their uncomfortable Channel crossing in seas which swamped ten landing craft as well as most of the overloaded DUKWs and DD Shermans, the 'green' troops of the 116th Regiment failed to achieve a great deal. One of Gerow's staff officers, Colonel Benjamin Talley, reported back to him on the morning of 6 June that the landing craft were swanning around 'like a stampeded herd of cattle' off the beach. Once the ordeal at 'Omaha' was behind them, though, the infantry of the 29th showed they were as good as the rest with battle honours including St Lô and Jülich (on the Rur north of Monschau).

V Corps itself broke out of the Normandy beachhead after taking a hammering during the German counter-attack at Mortain, then participated in the encirclement of the German Panzer divisions in the Falaise pocket, and drove on to Paris. This is where Gerow made his famous faux pas by attempting to deny General Jacques Leclerc's French 2nd Armoured Division the glory of entering the city at the head of the liberation forces. After an impassioned appeal from Leclerc, Bradley overruled Gerow and Gallic pride was appeased.

Gerow's Corps pressed on into Belgium across the Meuse and took part in the costly battles for Aachen and the Hürtgen Forest before ending up on the Rur river line in November. It had seen many changes in its composition during this time, due to the extremely flexible U.S. Corps system, and had long since lost the 29th Infantry Division to XIX Corps of Ninth Army.

Following the major reorganisation of the Army as a whole authorised on 24 December 1942 and implemented during 1943, sweeping changes took place at all levels of command to enhance strategic and tactical versatility. These changes extended from the highest level to the lowest, with logistic support becoming much more of an Army then a Corps concern, leaving Corps' commanders (with smaller staffs) better able to concentrate almost solely on the tactical disposition of the divisions and other units assigned to them.

Traditionally, the Corps system as devised by Napoleon provided a coherent mixed-arms force capable of taking on a superior enemy for a limited time until reinforced or relieved. To a large extent the U.S. Corps system in 1944 adhered to this principle, with a typical balance of two or three infantry divisions, one armoured division, a mechanised cavalry group, a field artillery brigade, one anti-aircraft and two engineer combat regiments, a tank destroyer group and a signals battalion; the armoured division was an operational 'extra' because the Allies did not deliberately create anything equivalent to the German Panzer Korps.

However, the U.S. Corps itself was much more a convenient administrative label used for planning purposes than a constant, coherent, grand tactical formation. Thus, divisions were swapped between Corps with regularity as one was taken out of the line

to recuperate and another, fresher, division taken from an adjoining Corps to compensate or counter-act a sudden threat. This accounts for much of the common confusion to the reader when studying the 'battle of the bulge', because divisions which were fighting as part of one Corps on the first page of an account are often ascribed to another on the subsequent page.

In this way, during the Ardennes conflict, Gerow

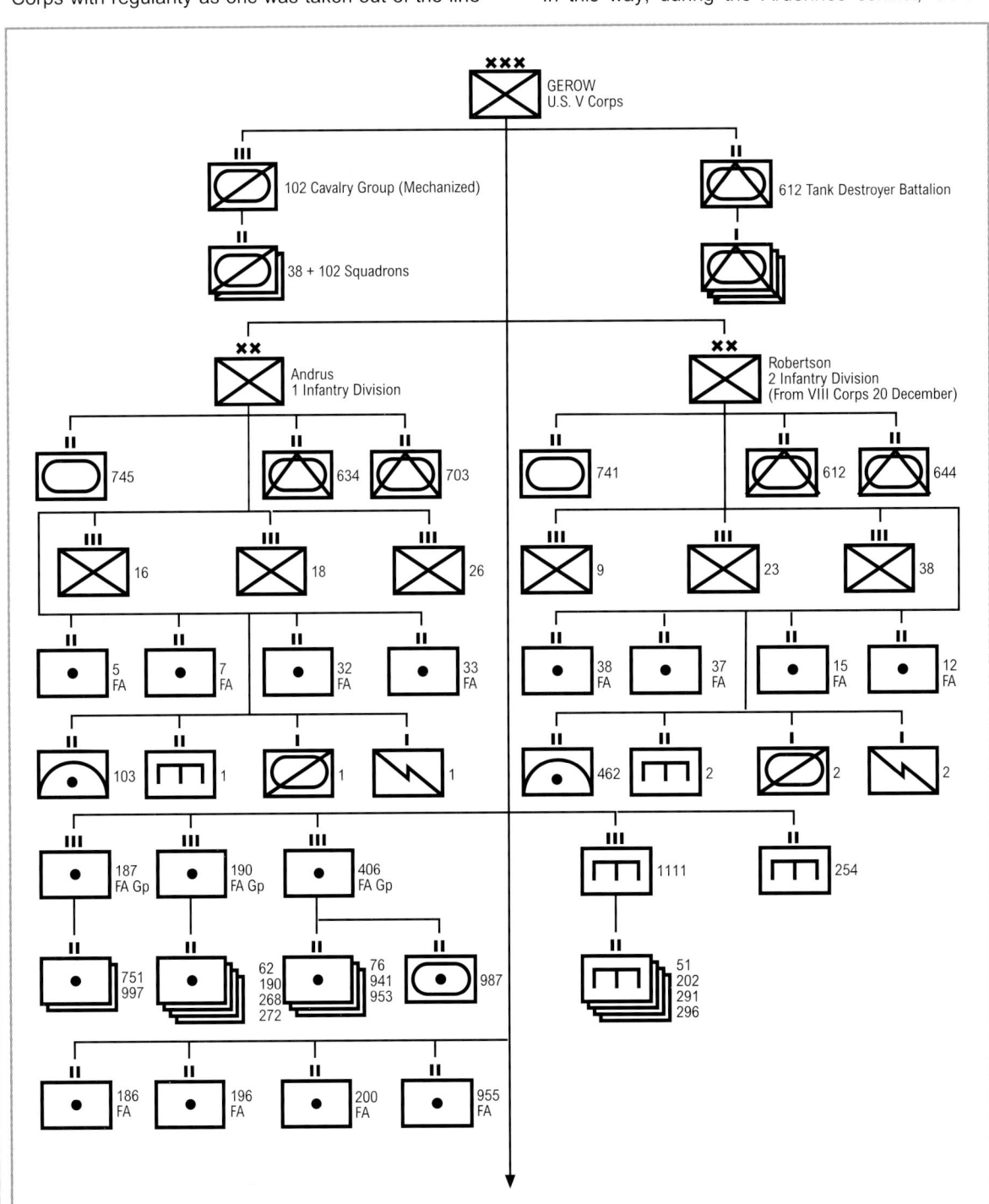

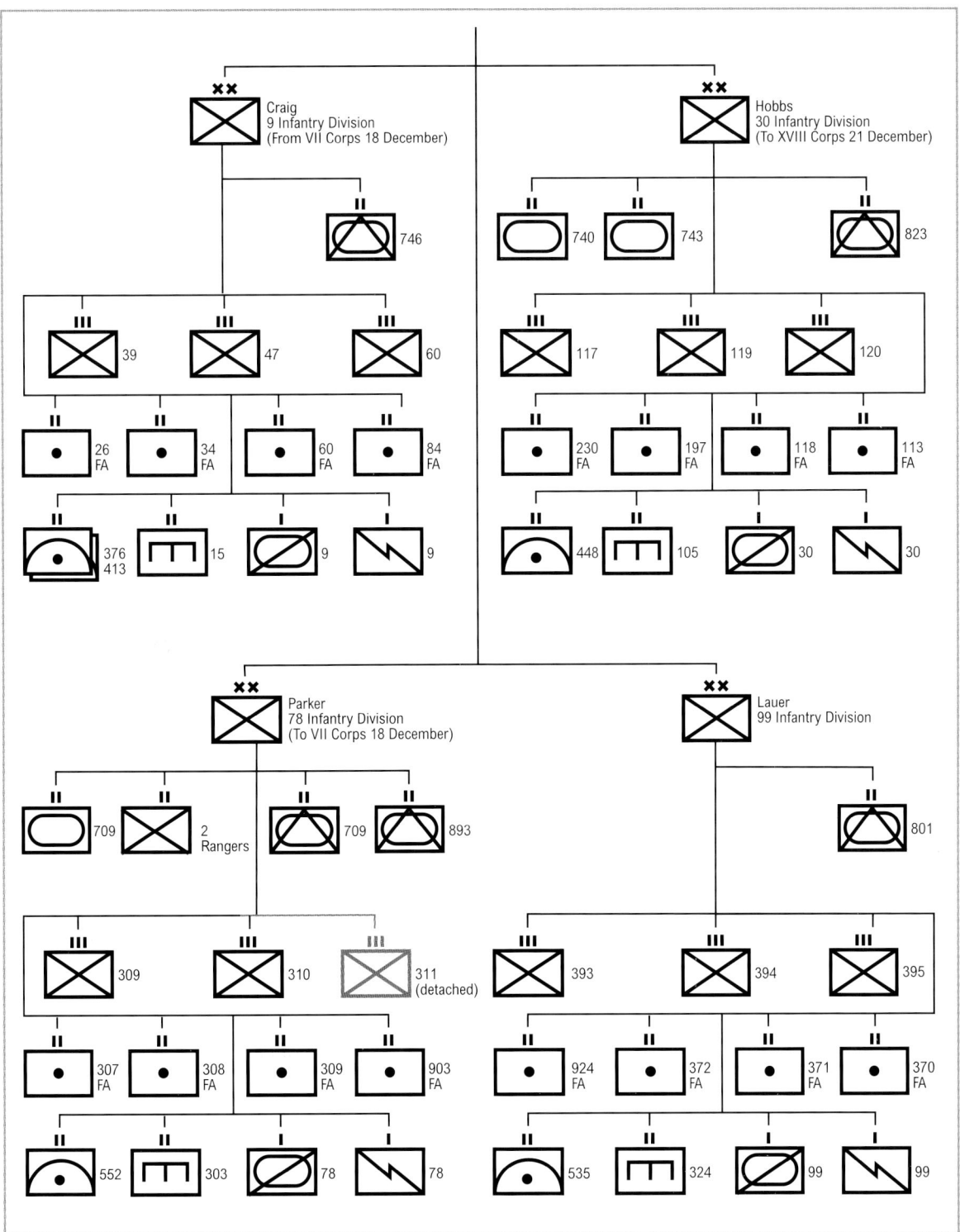

received the 1st and 9th Infantry Divisions from VII Corps, had temporary administrative responsibility for 2nd Armored Division on its way to VII Corps from 20-23 December, took over the 2nd Infantry Division from VIII Corps, and swapped his 78th Infantry Division with 30th Infantry Division from XIX Corps of Ninth Army, but then passed this on to XVIII (Airborne) Corps. In fact, only the 99th Infantry Division remained under Gerow's command during the whole battle, and even that went to VII Corps in February 1945.

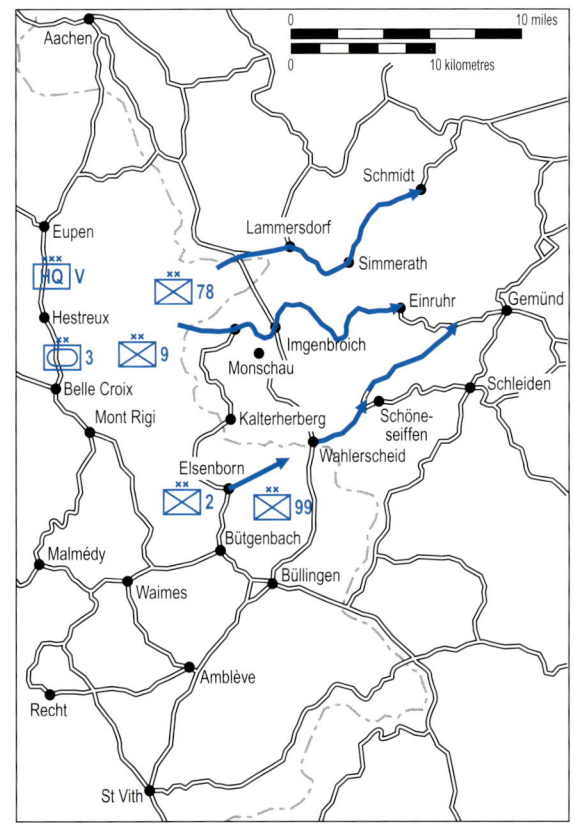

The planned V Corps' attack towards the Rur and Urft dams which began on 13 December was quickly called off in response to the German offensive, but fortuitously placed four divisions in a position from which they could be redeployed rapidly.

On 16 December V Corps actually had *tactical* control over, from north to south, the 78th, 9th and 99th Infantry Divisions, plus 3rd Armored 'on loan' from VII Corps which would quickly revert to Collins' command after passing through XVIII (Airborne) Corps territory over 19-22 December. These were the forces amass-ed for Hodges' planned attack north and south of Monschau to seize the Rur and Urft dams, together with the 2nd Infantry Division which was still part of Troy Middleton's VIII Corps, itself to Gerow's south, in the Schnee Eifel. For all its flexibility, the U.S. Corps system did lead to many unnecessary confusions in the chain of command which themselves led to unfortunate delays in responding to the German threat when men less positive than Gerow were unable to be decisive. 'Wrong decision, right time,' often works better in warfare, as much as in business, than 'right decision, too late'.

To begin with, V Corps' attack which began on 13 December looked as though it was going to plan,

but next day the 78th ran into opposition from 272 Volksgrenadier Division which counter-attacked at Rollsbroich and Kesternich on the 15th, and the 2nd encountered 326 Volksgrenadier Division at Wahler-scheid (this being the first indication the Allies had that this division was in that sector of the front at all).

The failure of Allied intelligence to spot the build-up of German forces or identify the units facing V and VIII Corps was very nearly the undoing of First Army. All that was believed to be in the line opposite Gerow's Corps was two, or possibly three, Volksgrenadier divisions of dubious fighting quality. One of these was known to be the 272nd and the other believed to be the 18th further south, with probably one more in between these two. The combination of the lack of 'Ultra' intercepts coupled with fragmentary German signals overheard in clear had led SHAEF planners to believe that the bulk of the German reserves were further north, with I SS-Panzer Korps somewhere northwest of Köln and II SS-Panzer Korps a little to its south, east of Jülich. In fact, Gerow was faced by three corps totalling nine divisions, four of them armoured, which should by rights have broken through the lines of the 99th Infantry Division with impunity.

If Gerow had known this, he could have been forgiv-en for panicking, but as it was he reacted with professional instinct to the threat. By midmorning on the 16th, with fragmentary reports of other German attacks coming in from VIII Corps, he was convinced that he was facing something more substantial than just a German reaction to the Americans' own Rur offensive. If he was right, he reasoned, the 2nd Infantry Division was out on a limb, while the 'green' 99th might be unable to cope with the situation. He telephoned Hodges at First Army headquarters in Spa and asked for permission to begin pulling the 2nd Infantry Division back towards the Elsenborn ridge. Hodges refused to give up V Corps' attack but Gerow nevertheless warned Major-General Walter Robert-son, the 2nd's CO, not to commit any more of his forces and to be prepared to turn them round. He also ordered him to release his reserve 23rd Infantry Regiment and send one battalion to Hünningen and the other to Krinkelt-Rocherath. That evening Robertson also received a telephone call from Hodges' deputy, Major-General Clarence Huebner (commander of 1st Infantry Division on D-Day), alerting him to be prepared to withdraw, and on the morning of the 17th, Hodges finally relented and told Gerow to act as he saw fit.

Forewarned, the experienced Robertson was able to respond rapidly from his command post in Wirtzfeld. First though, receiving reports of German armour

As earlier in the Hürtgen Forest, the battle in the Ardennes often turned into individual skirmishes between small squads of infantry probing cautiously for each other in an almost surreal environment.
(U.S. Signal Corps)

approaching Büllingen from his II/23rd Infantry Regiment near Hünningen, he was as amazed as anyone when the tanks – actually part of Kampfgruppe 'Peiper' – turned away southwest after resupplying themselves from the fuel depot there. Next Robertson began urgently pulling his regiments back in 'leapfrog' fashion, using the 395th Regiment of the 99th Infantry Division to provide cover for the withdrawal of the 9th Regiment (which had suffered heavy casualties at Wahlerscheid). The manoeuvre was a success although there was a great deal of confusion over the next 24 hours as Robertson – having been given command of the 99th as well as his own 2nd by Gerow – consolidated on Elsenborn ridge while the battalions of the 99th pulled back through their ranks, sometimes closely intermingled with advancing German grenadiers.

With this flank now secure, and Major-General Clift Andrus' 1st Infantry Division released from VII Corps to cover the mounting threat from 12 SS-Panzer Division at Büllingen-Dom Bütgenbach, Gerow could turn his attention to his western flank which was threatened by the slow advance of Kampfgruppe 'Peiper' and other elements of 1 SS-Panzer Division. To this task Gerow assigned Major-General Leland Hobbs' 30th Infantry Division, released to him from XIX Corps, Ninth Army, at Hodges' request. The energetic Hobbs promptly captured Stavelot, blocking Peiper's line of communication and retreat, held it against counter-attack from Kampfgruppe 'Knittel' and other form-ations, and forced Peiper to abandon Stoumont and fall back to La Gleize. There the German battlegroup was finally annihilated by 30th Infantry and 3rd Armoured Divisions from VII Corps.

By Christmas Day the German offensive had run out of steam and early in the New Year the Allies began to erase the 'bulge'. This was complete by the beginning of February and V Corps resumed its abandoned attack on the Rur and Urft dams, advanced to the Rhine, crossed at Remagen in March and ended the war in Austria.

V Corps' defence of the Allied northern shoulder had really rested on the shoulders of two men, Gerow and Robertson, who slowed I SS-Panzer Korps down sufficiently that engineers could blow the bridges to give time for stronger Allied reinforcements to arrive.

1st Infantry Division
'The Big Red One'

The 1st Infantry Division was enjoying a well-deserved rest, having been relieved by the 9th Infantry Division after 15 days of continuous combat in the Hürtgen Forest, when it was peremptorily despatched south from Meyrode through Eupen to the Malmédy region and thence to the assistance of the defenders on Elsenborn ridge. Hodges had already told the CO of VII Corps, Major-General Lawton Collins, to transfer the 16th Infantry Regiment to V Corps on 16 December, and the rest of the division followed suit over the 17th-19th. To many of the veterans in its ranks it felt like Kasserine revisited.

The division was already in existence at the beginning of the war and moved from Fort Hamilton, NY, to Fort Benning, Georgia, in November 1939. At the time of Pearl Harbor it was stationed at Fort Devens, Massachusetts. The 1st Infantry was one of the first U.S. Army divisions to see action, after being shipped to England at the beginning of August 1942 under the command of Major-General Terry de la Mesa Allen. It then joined a convoy heading for North Africa and landed unopposed near Oran in Algeria on 8 November as part of Major-General Lloyd Fredendall's Center Task Force in operation 'Torch'. The division made slow but steady progress during its first weeks in Africa but German resistance stiffened. In January 1943, Generaloberst Jürgen von Arnim's Fifth Panzer Armee launched a number of limited but successful counter-attacks against the French XIX Corps through the Pichon Pass, and Rommel audaciously suggested these could be followed up by a further assertive thrust a little to the south, out of Tunisia through the Kasserine Pass towards Tebéssa in Algeria with the intention of splitting his enemies and driving north to Bône on the coast, cutting off all the Allied forces then in Tunisia.

The operation launched on Valentine's Day 1943 was thus a mirror image of what was to happen later in the Ardennes, albeit on a smaller scale. The main blow landed on Fredendall's inexperienced II Corps on the inland sector of the Allied line, which fell back in disorder. 1st Armored Division's CCA lost 44 tanks on day one and when CCC counter-attacked on the 15th it lost another 58, nearly half the division's tanks in two days. It was into this inferno that 1st Infantry Division, together with other American and British formations, was rushed on the 17th/18th.

1st INFANTRY DIVISION
Major-General Clift Andrus
HQ Company

---

16 Infantry Regiment (Gibb)
18 Infantry Regiment
26 Infantry Regiment (Seitz)
5 Field Artillery Battalion
7 Field Artillery Battalion
32 Field Artillery Battalion
33 Field Artillery Battalion
1 Reconnaissance Troop, Mechanized
1 Engineer Combat Battalion
1 Medical Battalion
1 Signal Company
1 Quartermaster Company
701 Ordnance Light Maintenance Company
103 Anti-Aircraft Artillery Auto-Weapons Battalion (attached)
745 Tank Battalion (attached)
634 Tank Destroyer Battalion (attached)
703 Tank Destroyer Battalion (attached 18 December)

The Allied ground commander, General Sir Harold Alexander, visited Fredendall's headquarters and was so shocked by the confusion he found there that he persuaded Eisenhower to appoint Major-General Ernest N. Harmon (later CO of 2nd Armored Division in the Ardennes) to take effective charge. Fortunately, the German assault was contained and Rommel called the operation off on the 22nd, but American confidence had been severely shaken.

After the battle of Kasserine the Allies renewed their offensive although the 1st Infantry Division only just managed to contain further counter-attacks east of El Guettar during 23-28 March and had to halt its advance on Gabes. It met heavy opposition in April along the Medjez el Bab-Tunis road, but German resistance was crumbling and their last troops surrendered on 13 May.

The 1st Infantry Division landed at Gela, Sicily, on 10 July, and fought with distinction during the Allied conquest of the island, winning bloody battles against the 'Hermann Göring' and 15 Panzergrenadier Divisions. The 1st division, now commanded by Major-General Clarence R. Huebner, debarked from Sicily on

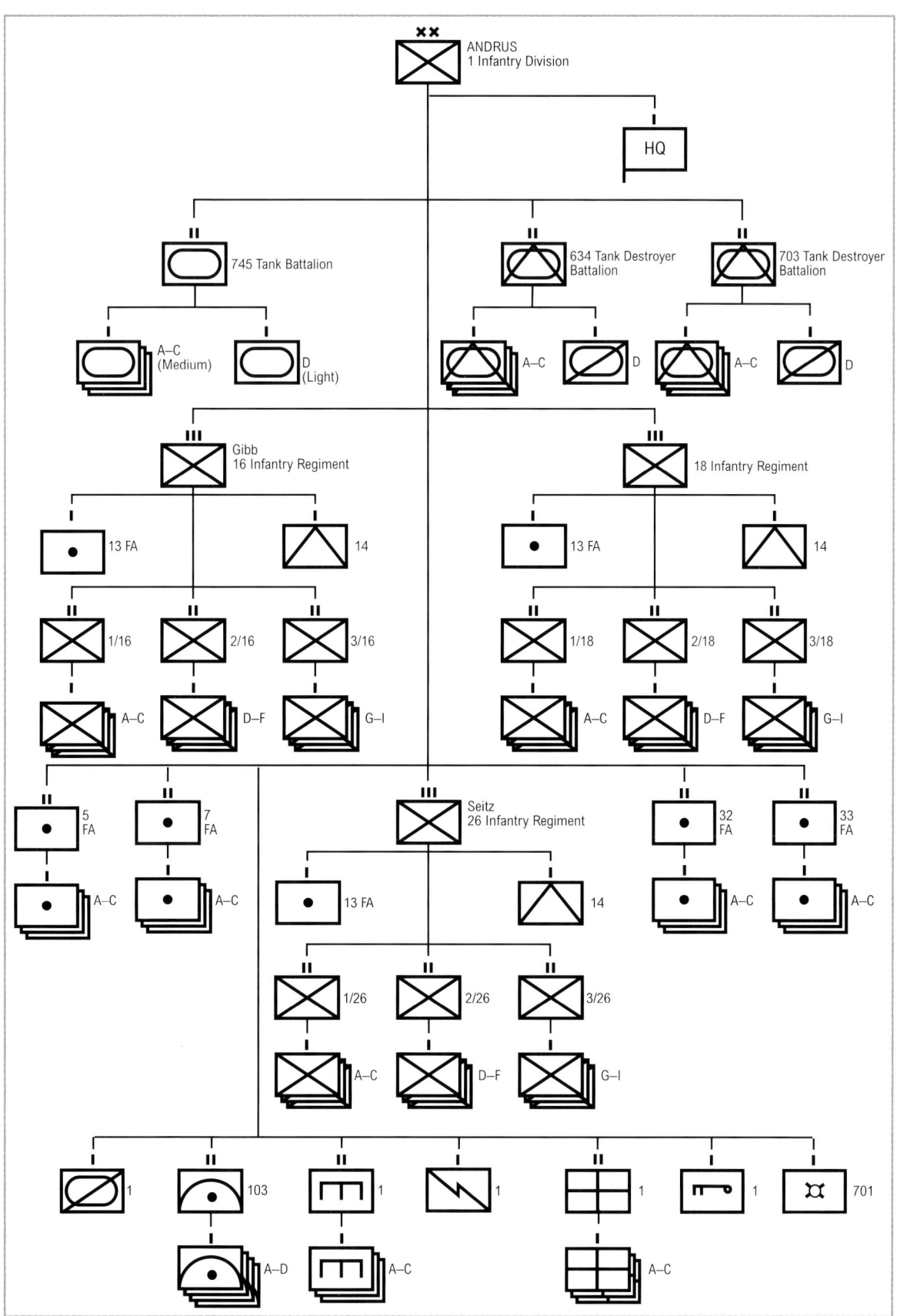

Colonel John Seitz's 26th Infantry Regiment arrived in the vicinity of Dom Bütgenbach just in time to counter a possible German outflanking manoeuvre around the southwest edge of Elsenborn ridge.

(U.S. Signal Corps)

23 October, en route to England to begin training for D-Day.

Transferred to Leonard Gerow's V Corps, U.S. First Army, it came ashore on 6 June 1944 at 'bloody Omaha' beach where it faced the tough 352 Infanterie Division (which would form part of LXXXV Korps, Seventh Armee, in the Ardennes). 'Omaha' was the division's sternest test. The cold, seasick men, burdened down with waterlogged equipment, only just managed to claw a fingerhold on the beach in face of intense artillery and machine-gun fire.

Over the next few days V Corps steadily extended its beachhead. Following the breakout from Normandy the division then fought at Mons at the beginning of September and crossed the Meuse at Liège on the 9th. It was next heavily involved in the costly siege of Aachen, battling this time against 246 Volksgrenadier Division which would also be encountered in the Ardennes. Aachen finally fell after vicious house-to-house fighting on 21 October.

The 1st Infantry Division spearheaded First Army's offensive through the Hürtgen Forest towards the River Rur on 16 November but after over a fortnight of continuous fighting had only managed to advance four miles so was pulled out of the line again over 5-7 December. With Huebner appointed as

Gerow's deputy, command of the division passed to Major-General Clift Andrus for the remainder of the war. Rushed south over 17-19 December to help out on Elsenborn ridge, 1st Infantry halted 12 SS-Panzer Division at Dom Bütgenbach, even though its lines were broken once on the 22nd. This finally destroyed all German chances of a breakthrough in the northern sector of the front and on 15 January 1945 the 1st Infantry Division forced open a door to enable 7th Armored Division to retake St Vith. It resumed its advance on the West Wall on 28 January before being relieved once more on 5 February.

After a brief respite outside Aywaille, during which replacements ('reinforcements') were assimilated for some of the division's casualties, the 1st replaced the 8th Infantry Division on the Rur and the 16th Regiment initiated the attack across the river at Kreuznau on 25 February, following up across the Neffel on 7 March. Bonn fell to the division after a brief two-day battle on the 9th which ended German resistance on the west bank of the Rhine. The 1st crossed over on 15 March but ran into tough opposition as it approached the River Sieg and needed all three of its regiments in line to capture Seigen.

Relieved itself now by the 8th Infantry Division, the 1st helped seal the Ruhr pocket at Paderborn and on 8 April forced a crossing of the River Weser for 3rd Armored Division. After clearing up pockets of resistance in the foothills of the Harz Mountains, the division ended the war on the Czech border near Karlsbad. Total casualties amounted to 3,616 killed – nearly a third of them at 'Omaha' beach – and 15,208 wounded.

2nd Infantry Division

'Indianhead'

For the men of Major-General Walter M. Robertson's 2nd Infantry Division, the battle of the Ardennes began on 13, not 16, December 1944, when V Corps opened a new offensive against the Rur and Urft dams. SHAEF had belatedly realised, in the wake of the severe flooding which had so hampered operations around Antwerp, that all the Germans had to do was open the dams' floodgates, or dynamite them, to turn the whole region east of Monschau into a virtually impassable quagmire. To prevent this, Gerow was sending in the 2nd Infantry Division to outflank Monschau from the southwest

Major-General Walter M. Robertson was awarded the Bronze Star for his spirited defence in front of Elsenborn ridge.

(U.S. Signal Corps)

2nd INFANTRY DIVISION
Major-General Walter M. Robertson
HQ Company

9 Infantry Regiment (Hirschfelder)
23 Infantry Regiment (Loveless)
38 Infantry Regiment (Boos)
12 Field Artillery Battalion
15 Field Artillery Battalion
37 Field Artillery Battalion
38 Field Artillery Battalion
2 Reconnaissance Troop, Mechanized
2 Engineer Combat Battalion
2 Medical Battalion
2 Signal Company
2 Quartermaster Company
702 Ordnance Light Maintenance Company
462 Anti-Aircraft Artillery Auto-Weapons Battalion (attached)
741 Tank Battalion (Skaggs) (attached)
612 Tank Destroyer Battalion (attached)
644 Tank Destroyer Battalion (attached)

while the 9th Infantry Division (which had just relieved the 1st) advanced in the centre accompanied by 3rd Armored Division, and the 78th Infantry Division converged from the northwest.

The 2nd Infantry Division had been positioned in the Schnee Eifel east of St Vith since the end of September. It was a quiet part of the front where nothing happened except for some desultory artillery fire and an occasional contact with German patrols, but since early December the sentries had scarcely had a minor skirmish to alleviate the cold and boredom. That changed on 11 December when the division vacated its familiar foxholes and dugouts, for the 106th Infantry Division, a fresh unit which had so for seen no action, and moved to Camp Elsenborn.

Robertson was an experienced commander who knew his men faced a difficult task, because few people had not heard the tales of horror from the battles in the Hürtgen Forest. Robertson himself came from an old Virginia family and had graduated from West Point in 1912. He saw no action during World

War 1 but served as an instructor at both the Staff and the War College during the interwar period. He had a relaxed manner and was slow to anger, but his temper when roused matched his red hair. He did not often drink or socialise, but was respected both by his fellow officers and the men whom he commanded.

Robertson took over the 2nd Infantry Division at Fort Sam Houston, Texas, from Major-General John C. Lee in May 1942, but his hopes of early involvement in the war were disappointed. The division he commanded until after the end of the conflict in Europe did not arrive in England until October 1943 when it began intensive training for D-Day. Assigned to Gerow's V Corps alongside the 1st Infantry Division which was to assault 'Omaha' beach, Robertson's men did not face the same ordeal as Huebner's, travelling ashore in relative comfort on D+1, 7 June 1944.

Gerow did not waste any time getting the 2nd Infantry Division into action once it was finally ashore. It advanced inland and was involved in the capture of St Lô and the siege of Brest in Brittany. The port was

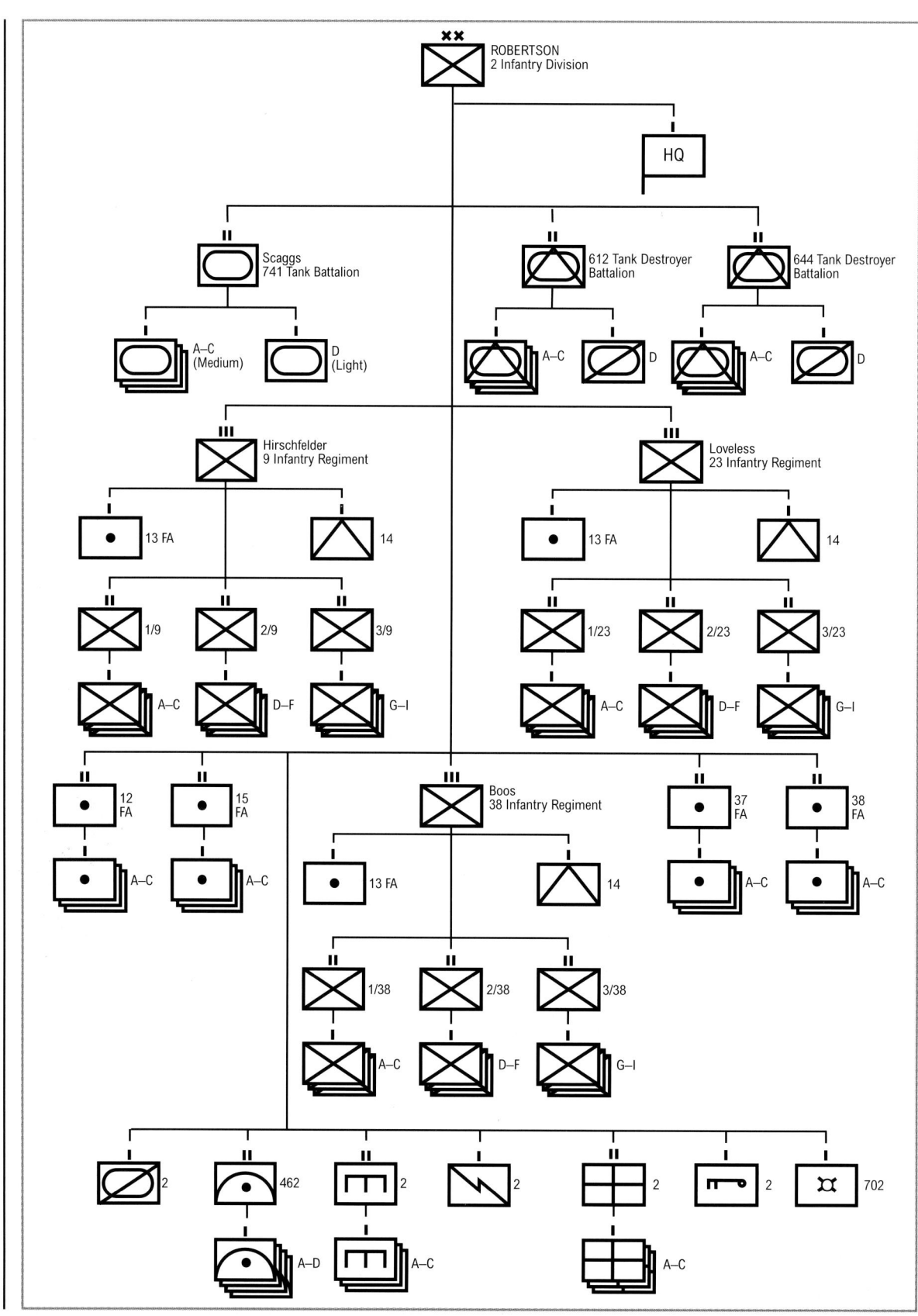

Major-General Leonard Gerow, left, was able to pin a Bronze Star on Walter Robertson's chest after he had salvaged the perilous situation around Krinkelt-Rocherath. (U.S. Signal Corps)

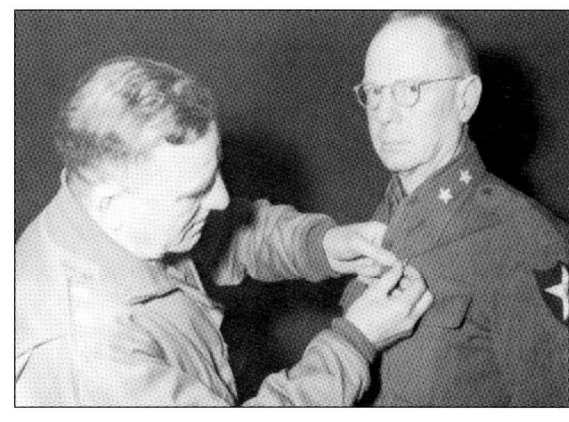

defended by Fallschirmjäger under the very capable Generalmajor Bernard Ramcke and did not fall until 18 September.

A week later the division entrained for St Vith, still as part of VIII Corps although it would revert to V Corps for the 'battle of the bulge'. Duly rested after all they had been through, Robertson's men accepted their new assignment on 13 December with stoicism. Their commander was less phlegmatic, because their route from Camp Elsenborn towards their first objective, Wahlerscheid – a fortified part of the West Wall – lay at the end of a nightmare trek along a narrow track, undeserving of the name 'road' despite all the efforts of Lieutenant-Colonel Robert W. Warren's 2nd Engineer Combat Battalion over the preceding couple of days. This passed behind the positions of the 99th Infantry Division in front of Elsenborn ridge, and Robertson feared that a decisive German attack on this 'green' division could sever his column and decimate his command. Fortunately, it did not happen, and the division's 9th Regiment captured Wahlerscheid during the night of 15 December while its garrison was still half asleep.

When the German onslaught all down the line of the Schnee Eifel opened a few hours later, 2nd Infantry Division was out on a limb and would not resume its offensive towards the Rur and Urft dams until 1 February 1945. Instead, it was pulled back to help the 99th Infantry Division on Elsenborn ridge, with Robertson given overall command. After the crisis was past, the 2nd Infantry Division finally crossed the Rur on 3 March 1945, then the Rhine at Remagen on the 21st. Further fierce fighting followed in April, particularly crossing the River Weser, but the division captured Leipzig on the 19th and ended the war outside Pilsen. Casualties in less than a year's action totalled 3,031 killed and 12,785 wounded.

Men of Colonel Francis Boos' 38th Infantry Regiment retrace their footsteps through the snow towards Krinkelt on 17 December. (U.S. Signal Corps)

9th Infantry Division

'Octofoil'

Even as the German assault opened on 16 December 1944, Major-General Louis Craig's 9th Infantry Division was already in action against one of Sixth Panzer Armee's formations, 272 Volksgrenadier Division, to the north of Monschau. In concert with 3rd Armored Division, and with the 78th and 2nd Infantry Divisions on either flank, the 9th had begun moving up for First Army's attack towards the Rur and Urft dams on 10 December, and had struck the right flank of Generalleutnant Otto Hitzfeld's LXVII Korps. Transferred to V Corps on 18 December, and leaving his 60th Infantry Regiment to continue pinning down the Volksgrenadiers, Craig brought his 39th and 47th Regiments south towards Elsenborn ridge where they were largely instrumental in defeating the last attacks of 3 Panzergrenadier Division. The 9th then relieved the battered 2nd and 99th Infantry Divisions on the ridge and established a solid line of defence between Kalterherberg and Elsenborn which it held until 30 January 1945.

Alongside the 1st Infantry Division, the 9th held one of the longest combat records of the war and had already won several battle honours. Activated at Fort Bragg under Colonel Charles B. Elliot on 1 August 1940, it had three changes of commander over the next two years before Major-General Manton S. Eddy took over in August 1942. During the interim the division had taken part in the major Carolina manoeuvres in autumn 1941 and received intensive training in seaborne assault techniques with the Atlantic Fleet Amphibious Corps in 1942. At the time Eddy took over, the division had already been earmarked for operation 'Torch', the invasion of French northwest Africa.

In the end, only the infantry regiments took part in the operation, the 60th encountering stiff French resistance at Port Lyautey airfield inland from Mehdia. The division did not fight as a whole until the end of March 1943 but triumphantly entered Bizerta on 8 May and was then involved in the latter stages of the battle for Sicily in July-August. Soon afterwards it was in England to prepare for D-Day but, despite its previous specialised training in amphibious assault, the division did not land in France across 'Utah' beach as part of VII Corps until 10 June.

The 9th's principal assignment was to seal off the base of the Cotentin peninsula, which it accomplished

---

9th INFANTRY DIVISION
Major-General Louis A. Craig
HQ Company

---

39 Infantry Regiment
47 Infantry Regiment
60 Infantry Regiment
26 Field Artillery Battalion
34 Field Artillery Battalion
60 Field Artillery Battalion
84 Field Artillery Battalion
9 Reconnaissance Troop, Mechanized
15 Engineer Combat Battalion
9 Medical Battalion
9 Signal Company
9 Quartermaster Company
709 Ordnance Light Maintenance Company
376 Anti-Aircraft Artillery Auto-Weapons Battalion (attached)
413 Anti-Aircraft Artillery Auto-Weapons Battalion
    (attached 20 December)
746 Tank Destroyer Battalion (attached)

---

on 17 June, and then to capture the port of Cherbourg to relieve the pressure on the 'Mulberry' harbours. The division took the final German surrender here on 29 June, then joined the breakout from Normandy in July and helped both seal the Falaise pocket and repel the counter-attack at Mortain in August.

Now accompanying 3rd Armored Division, the 9th crossed the River Marne and joined 12th Army Group's headlong 'broad front' pursuit of the rapidly retreating German forces all the way to the Meuse by the beginning of September. By this time it had a new commander, Louis Craig, because Manton Eddy had been promoted to lead XII Corps further south. On the Meuse, the 9th faced strong opposition at Dinant but forced a crossing on 6 September, captured Huy to the north then mopped up the remaining German forces in Liège. From now on, though, the resistance got tougher as the 47th Regiment drove east to the West Wall, capturing Kalterherberg on the 14th while the 39th seized Lammersdorf and the 60th Höfen, putting Monschau on the River Rur in a tight noose.

During the remainder of September, the whole of

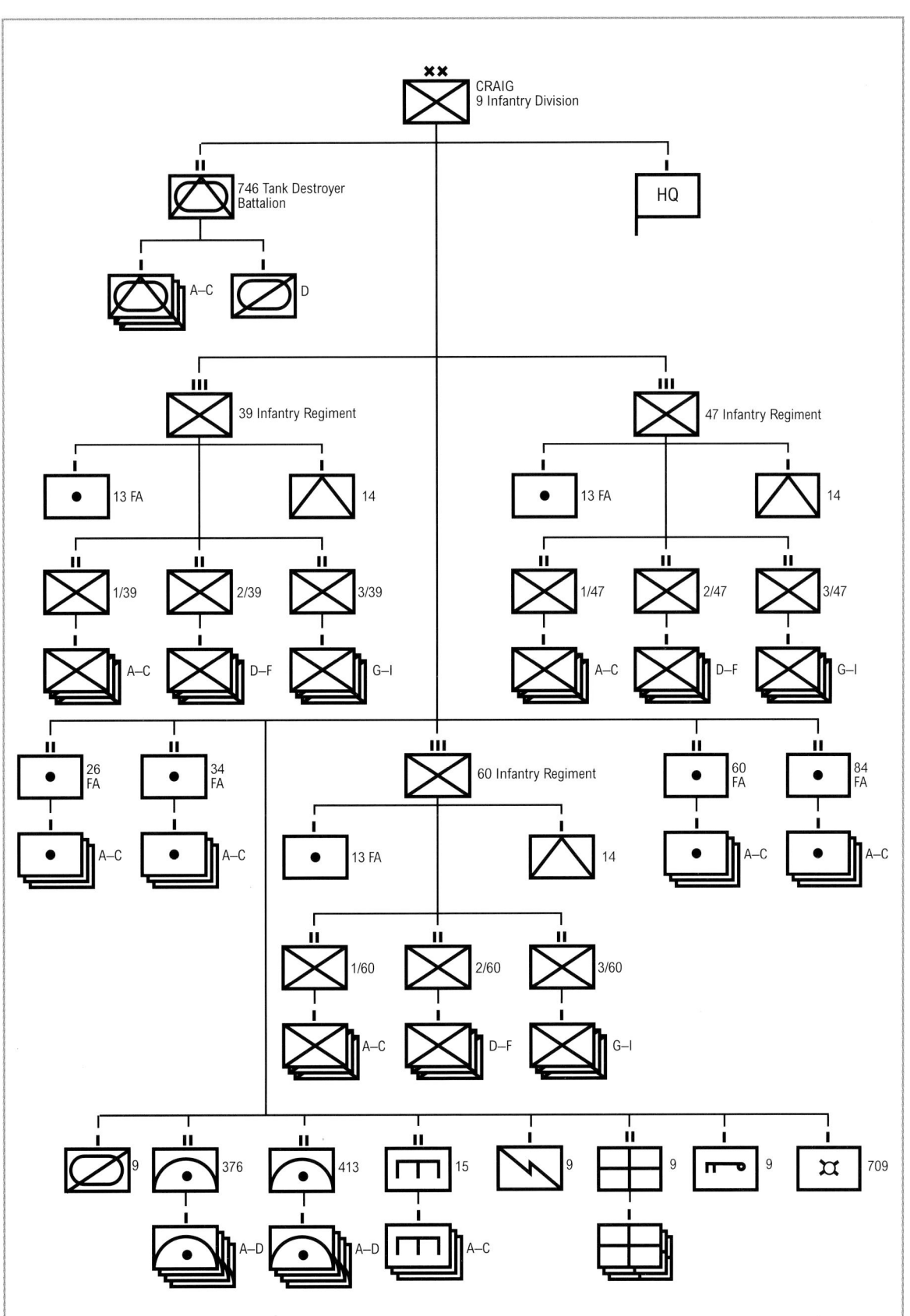

A rifleman of the 9th Infantry Division takes a pot-shot at a rare German aircraft. Small-arms fire was almost totally ineffectual in such a situation but was a great boost to morale.
(U.S. Signal Corps)

October and into the middle of November, all three of the 9th's infantry regiments endured the torment of the Hürtgen Forest, a nightmare landscape populated largely, according to myth, by trolls, but which, in reality, concealed well-armed and well-motivated German grenadiers in every fold of the ground and behind each tree. The fighting was often at very close quarters and gave many men on both sides nightmares for years afterwards.

Relief was shortlived in December because the 9th was next assigned to take part in the offensive to capture the Rur and Urft dams, but found itself acting as a breakwater on Elsenborn ridge instead. The postponed attack did not resume for the 9th until 1 February 1945, when the 39th and 60th Infantry Regiments reached Dreiborn and the 47th the high ground overlooking Hammer. There was fierce house-to-house fighting here and elsewhere but the 47th Regiment had the satisfaction of taking

Wollseifen then capturing one of the minor dams on the Urft reservoir intact within a week. The division was now reinforced by the 309th and 311th Regiments from the adjacent 78th Infantry Division and captured the major Schwammenauel Dam on 9 February, then it was back to the Hürtgen Forest for a mopping-up operation which went on until nearly the end of the month.

The 9th Infantry Division recrossed the Rur on 26-28 February and pushed towards Thum and Berg. Now accompanying 9th Armored Division in its drive towards the Rhine, 9th Infantry benefited from the latter's fortuitous capture of the Ludendorff railway bridge at Remagen. After helping to defend the bridge-head against local counter-attacks, 9th Infantry Division, led by the 60th Regiment, followed 9th Armored's advance into Germany 'proper', crossed the River Lied and at the beginning of April helped seal the Ruhr pocket. Alongside 1st Infantry Division it then helped clear the Harz Mountains and captured Mägdesprung, Friedrichsbrunn, Opperode and Quedlinburg.

The division ended the war near Dessau on the River Mulde, having suffered the equivalent of nearly 1,000 casualties a month since it first sailed from the U.S.A. in 1942.

The little 57mm M1 anti-tank gun issued to the infantry was an improved 50-cal version of the British 6-pdr. By 1944 it was little more than a 'door knocker' apart from the occasional fluke shot.
(U.S. Signal Corps)

30th Infantry Division

'Old Hickory'

Rather like the 2nd Infantry Division, the 30th could not call itself a real 'veteran' unit such as the 1st or 9th in December 1944 because it, too, had not seen combat in World War 2 until after the D-Day landings. However, consonant with its illustrious earlier history, the division very quickly made up the 'deficiency' and was largely instrumental in sealing the fate of Kampfgruppe 'Peiper' at La Gleize, Stoumont and Stavelot.

At the time the German onslaught opened, the 30th was temporarily unemployed behind the front line of

Major-General Leland S. Hobbs was a determined and resourceful CO who expected, and received, the very best from his men.
(U.S. Signal Corps)

30th INFANTRY DIVISION
Major-General Leland S. Hobbs
HQ Company

---

117 Infantry Regiment (Johnson)
119 Infantry Regiment (Sutherland)
120 Infantry Regiment
113 Field Artillery Battalion
118 Field Artillery Battalion
197 Field Artillery Battalion
230 Field Artillery Battalion
30 Reconnaissance Troop, Mechanized
105 Engineer Combat Battalion
105 Medical Battalion
30 Signal Company
30 Quartermaster Company
730 Ordnance Light Maintenance Company
448 Anti-Aircraft Artillery Auto-Weapons Battalion (attached)
551 Parachute Infantry Battalion (Joerg) (attached)
740 Tank Battalion (Rubel) (attached 19 December)
743 Tank Battalion (attached)
823 Tank Destroyer Battalion (attached)

---

the U.S. Ninth Army's planned attack across the River Rur around Jülich but, like the 2nd and 7th Armored Divisions which *were* involved in this attack, it was speedily moved south to help contain I SS-Panzer Korps' assault. Temporarily assigned to V Corps, First Army, it was reassigned to XVIII (Airborne) Corps four days later, but played its most crucial part in the 'battle of the bulge' during its opening phase.

Originally a Carolinas-Tennessee National Guard formation, and taking its nickname from President Andrew Jackson, the division was taken into federal service at Fort Jackson, South Carolina, on 16 September 1940 under Major-General Henry D. Russell. For a brief period during 1942 it was co-mmanded by Major-General William H. Simpson – CO of Ninth Army in December 1944 – but from September 1942 until the same month in 1945 it was very ably led by Major-General Leland S. Hobbs. The division shipped from Boston to England in February 1944 as part of Major-General Charles H. Corlett's XIX Corps, with which it served for most of the war, and came

ashore in France across 'Omaha' beach on 10 June.

Moving quickly forward through Isigny with 2nd Armored on its right flank and the 35th Infantry Division to its left, the 30th met opposition mostly from Freiherr von der Heydte's 6 Fallschirmjäger Regiment south of Carentan on the line of the canal between the rivers Vire and Taute. XIX Corps launched a series of limited tactical attacks in this sector which were mainly intended to keep the Germans off-balance during the remainder of June.

During July the 30th was on XIX Corps' right flank and checked a German counter-attack on 11 July, crossed the Périers-St Lô highway and reached the River Vire at the beginning of August. Here it was only temporarily delayed by Panzer 'Lehr' Division near Mortain. The men of the 30th, all coming from the same part of the United States unlike those in most other divisions during World War 2, had a sense of unity and comradeship which contributed significantly to their fighting élan, and were now 'on a roll'. Following 2nd Armored Division, they entered Belgium

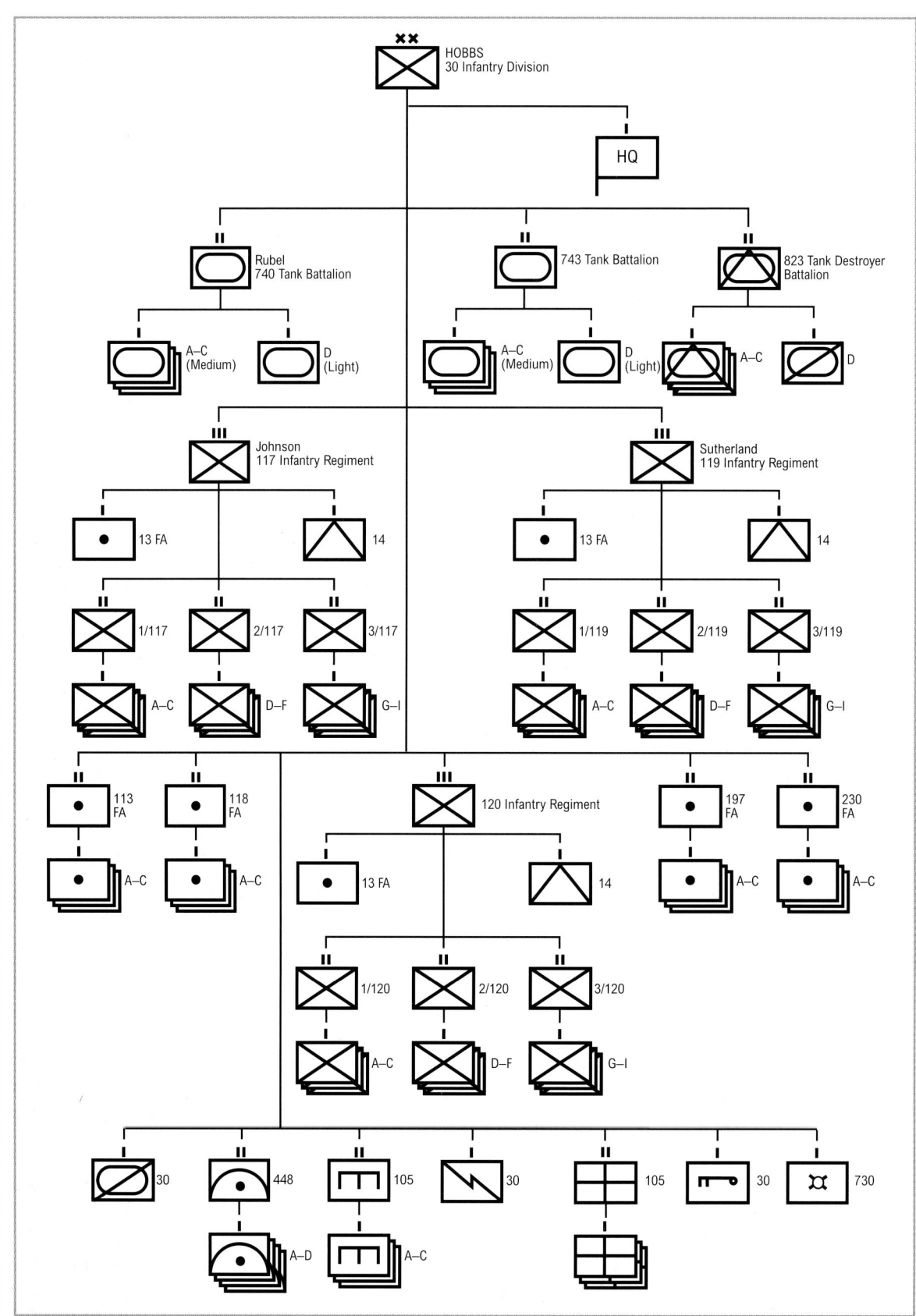

and crossed the Meuse near Liège on the 11th. Three days later they entered Maastricht then, crossing the German border reached Marienburg on 18 September. There was heavy fighting at Geilenkirchen in October and at Warden and Lohn in November, but in December the division was put into reserve to rest and refit so was strategically 'unemployed' when the Ardennes offensive began.

At this point the CO of First Army, Courtney Hodges, telephoned his longstanding friend and comrade in arms from World War 1, 'Bill' Simpson, to see whether he could 'borrow' the 30th. Simpson promptly telephoned Hobbs and told him to get his division cracking. He had no details and was told the emergency was probably only temporary – which, in a sense, it was, although the division did not revert to XIX Corps until February 1945.

Moved south of Malmédy, the division recaptured Stavelot behind Kampfgruppe 'Peiper', ruining German attempts to reinforce it, and blocked its further westward advance at Stoumont. After Peiper abandoned his hopeless position at La Gleize and led his remaining thousand men out of the American trap on Christmas Eve, Hobbs' division cleared the remnants

Street fighting in Stavelot on 20 December. These men, from Colonel Walter Johnson's 117th Regiment, carry M1 Garand rifles, one of which is fitted with a grenade launcher. (U.S. Signal Corps)

of Kampfgruppe 'Knittel' along the line of the River Amblève between Stavelot and Trois Ponts and began an eastward counter-attack on 13 January 1945.

Battlefields already familiar to other Allied divisions were recrossed at Recht, Born and Kaiserbaracke and the division was only two miles away from recapturing St Vith when it was pulled out of the line on 26 January. It reassembled at Lierneux then pulled back to the vicinity of Aachen to help in the renewed Allied offensive towards the Rur and Urft dams which the German assault had disrupted.

The 119th and 120th Regiments crossed the Rur near Schophoven on 23 February, and took Hanbach the following day while the 117th Regiment attacked Steinstrass. This cleared the path for 2nd Armored Division and the 30th again had a brief rest before being earmarked for the Rhine crossings in March. All three regiments abreast, it crossed the river in the Buderich-Rheinberg sector on 24 March and made contact with British Commandos the next day.

The 30th moved aside to let 8th Armored Division through its ranks and reassembled near Drenstein-fuhrt at the beginning of April. Attacking through the Teutoburger Wald, it crossed the River Weser and seized Hamelin, while its 117th Regiment captured Braunschweig. The 30th reached the agreed 'stop line' on the Elbe on 13 April, captured Magdeburg and made contact with leading elements of the Red Army on 5 May 1945.

78th Infantry Division

'Lightning'

Major-General Edwin Parker's 78th Infantry Division was almost totally inexperienced when the Germans launched operation 'Herbstnebel', only its 311th Regiment so far having seen any real action. The division had not been activated until 15 August 1942, at Camp Butner, North Carolina, and did not arrive in France until 22 November 1944. Unusually, it retained the same commander from inauguration until well after the end of the war in Europe.

Although the 78th had been in existence, and training had included taking part in the Carolina and Tennessee manoeuvres in 1943-44, it was one of those unfortunate infantry divisions whose ranks had been systematically stripped from time to time with its more-able recruits being shipped out to replace casualties in other units. This meant that when it did arrive in Europe, like other higher numbered divisions assigned to the Ardennes such an the 99th and 106th, many of its men had only undergone very basic training. Fortunately, the same was true of many of the Volksgrenadiers facing them.

Arriving in Belgium on 27 November, the division was first attached to XIX Corps but then transferred to V Corps on 5 December, taking over the sector of front recently vacated by the 1st Infantry Division. At this point the 311th Infantry Regiment was briefly detached to fight with Major-General Donald Stroh's 8th Infantry Division in the Hürtgen Forest, helping to eliminate a strong pocket of resistance to the south of Obermaubach.

The reunited division began its attack on the left flank of the offensive towards the Rur and Urft dams a week later, the 311th Regiment getting promptly involved in battle again against part of 272 Volksgrenadier Regiment, LXVII Korps, at Kesternich. This, together with 9th Infantry Division's simultaneous attack on the 78th's right flank, denied the Germans the use of this division in their own offensive.

Parker's division kept up the pressure at the junction between Sixth Panzer and Fifteenth Armees, clearing the high ground over the River Kall in the second week of January 1945 and finally capturing Kesternich on the 31st.

After mopping up this area, the 311th Regiment spearheaded the renewed drive across the flooded

---

78th INFANTRY DIVISION

Major-General Edwin P. Parker, Jr.

HQ Company

---

309 Infantry Regiment
310 Infantry Regiment
311 Infantry Regiment
  (detached to 8 Infantry Division on Rur river offensive)
307 Field Artillery Battalion
308 Field Artillery Battalion
309 Field Artillery Battalion
903 Field Artillery Battalion
78 Reconnaissance Troop, Mechanized
303 Engineer Combat Battalion
303 Medical Battalion
78 Signal Company
78 Quartermaster Company
778 Ordnance Light Maintenance Company
552 Anti-Aircraft Artillery Auto-Weapons Battalion
  (attached 20 December)
709 Tank Battalion (attached)
628 Tank Destroyer Battalion (attached 19 December)
893 Tank Destroyer Battalion (attached)

River Rur towards the Schwammenauel Dam. There was particularly heavy fighting for the little town of Schmidt over 7-9 February, during which the 309th and 311th Regiments briefly fell under 9th Infantry Division command, but the dam was captured on 9 February.

The 78th fought alongside the 9th during the renewed drive towards the Rhine at the end of the month and captured Heinbach, then crossed the river over the Ludendorff rail bridge at Remagen which had been miraculously captured intact by 9th Armored Division. The 309th and 311th Regiments were now again attached to 9th Infantry Division to help guard the bridgehead, while the 310th forced a crossing of the River Ahr at Löhndorf.

In mid-March the division attacked towards the main road between Frankfurt and Köln, fending off counter-attacks at Honnef and capturing Hovel and Königswinter on the 16th of the month. Advancing up the east bank of the Rhine, the 311th Infantry

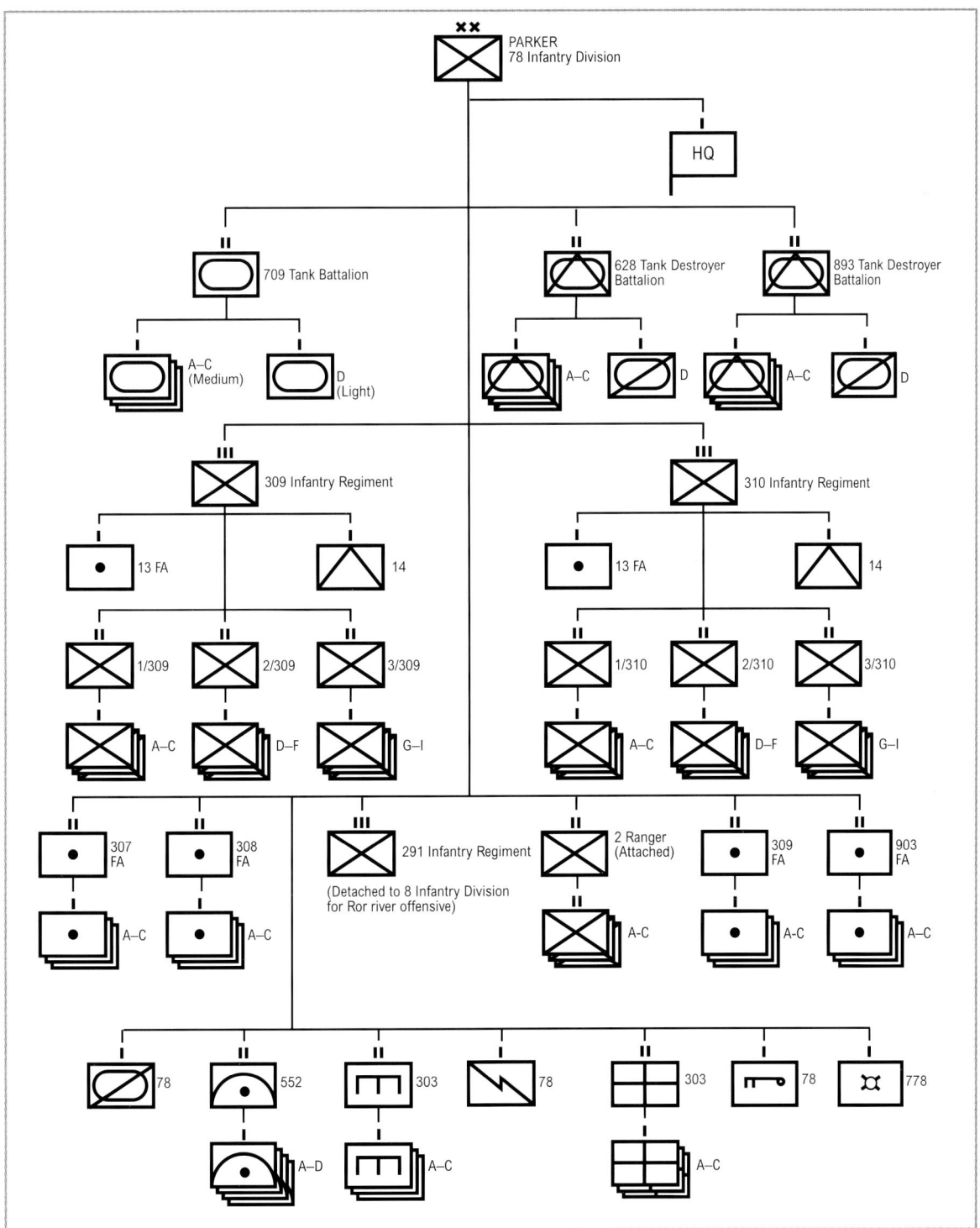

Regiment took Meindorf on the 21st, the 310th captured Menden on the 24th and the 309th subdued a strong pocket of resistance near Hennef on the 25th. After relieving the 1st Infantry Division on the south bank of the River Sieg at the end of the month, the 78th helped close the ring around the Ruhr pocket in April. Further battles were won at Waldbrol, Lichtenberg and Freudenberg, then the 78th assisted the 13th Armored Division at Wipperfürth before overrunning Elberfeld and Wuppertal. The division saw no further action, and ended the war on 7 May near Marbug.

99th Infantry Division
'Checkerboard'

Described by their own commander as the 'battle babies' in his book on their exploits, the men of the 99th Infantry Division were totally inexperienced when I SS-Panzer and LXVII Korps struck at dawn on 16 December. They had arrived in Europe only a month earlier and had been assigned what was regarded as a quiet sector of the front in which to get acclimatised. That they were able to withstand the onslaught until reinforced is more a tribute to sheer guts than to the quality of their training.

The division had been activated at Camp Van Dorn, Mississippi, on 15 November 1942, but did not ship to England until October 1944 and arrived in Belgium on 9 November. Its three infantry regiments, respectively the 395th, 393rd and 394th, were deployed in a shallow curve betwen Höfen in the north and Elsenborn to the south, and were well dug in with their artillery deployed to support the 2nd Infantry Division's attack through the West Wall towards the Rur and Urft dams. From 8-13 December work parties and engineers had been busy widening and surfacing the narrow north-south track through their positions to

99th INFANTRY DIVISION
Major-General Walter E. Lauer
HQ Company

393 Infantry Regiment (Scott)
394 Infantry Regiment (Riley)
395 Infantry Regiment (Mackenzie)
370 Field Artillery Battalion
371 Field Artillery Battalion
372 Field Artillery Battalion
924 Field Artillery Battalion
99 Reconnaissance Troop, Mechanized
324 Engineer Combat Battalion
324 Medical Battalion
99 Signal Company
99 Quartermaster Company
799 Ordnance Light Maintenance Company
535 Anti-Aircraft Artillery Auto-Weapons Battalion (attached)
801 Tank Destroyer Battalion (attached)
254 Engineer Combat Battalion (attached 17 December)

Major-General Walter E. Lauer had formerly commanded both the 66th and 80th Infantry Divisions before taking over the 99th in July 1943.

(U.S. Signal Corps)

facilitate the 2nd's advance, and this now came in doubly useful as the 2nd's attack was cancelled and the division was pulled back to reinforce the 99th in response to the German offensive.

Once this had been contained, the 99th received replacements in the line for the many men killed or wounded during the battle, and on 30 January 1945 the 393rd Regiment spearheaded the attack east of Elsenborn into the Monschau Forest.

The division was now pulled out of the line back to Waimes, apart from the 395th Regiment which lent

assistance to the 1st Infantry Division at Hellenthal over 3-5 February and then 3rd Armored Division at Pfaffendorf 1-3 March. The remainder of the division, spearheaded again by the 393rd, attacked across the River Erft towards Neurath on 2 March and reached the west bank of the Rhine at Grimlinghausen on the 5th.

The 99th crossed the Rhine at Remagen over the 10th-11th and helped consolidate the bridgehead, withstanding local counter-attacks and capturing Honnigen on the 16th. It then attacked behind 9th Armored Division across the River Wied, cutting the main road between Köln and Frankfurt on the 25th. It was now moved north for the assault on the Ruhr pocket and mopped up enemy strongpoints bypassed by 7th Armored Division at the beginning of April. The 99th captured Iserlohn on the 16th which caused German resistance to collapse in the eastern sector of the pocket.

Pushing on behind the 14th Armored Division, the 99th crossed the Danube and ended the war at Giesenhausen. In its short history the division lost 1,134 men.

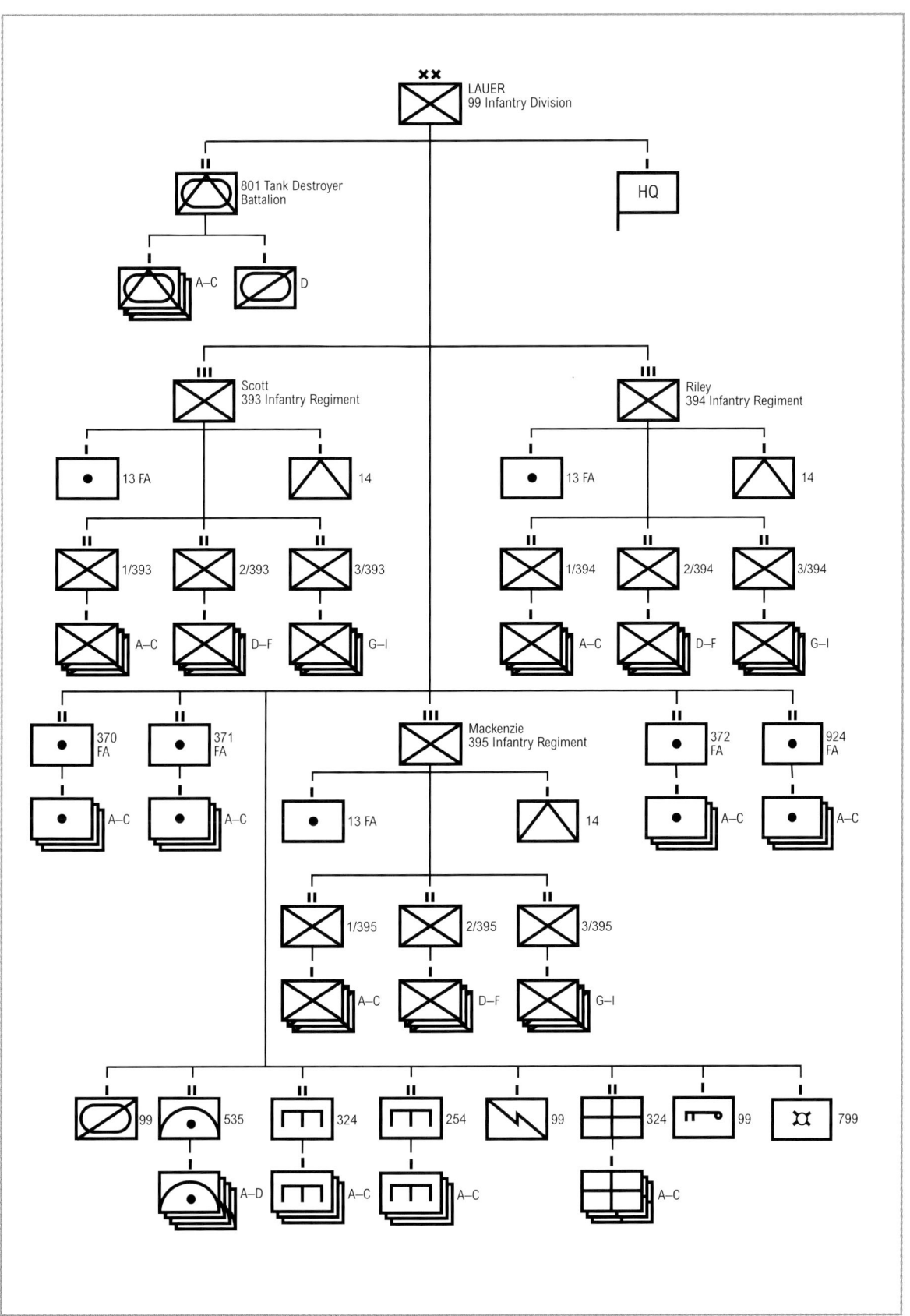

LAUER
99 Infantry Division

801 Tank Destroyer
Battalion

HQ

A–C

D

Scott
393 Infantry Regiment

Riley
394 Infantry Regiment

13 FA

14

13 FA

14

1/393

2/393

3/393

1/394

2/394

3/394

A–C

D–F

G–I

A–C

D–F

G–I

370
FA

371
FA

Mackenzie
395 Infantry Regiment

372
FA

924
FA

A–C

A–C

13 FA

14

A–C

A–C

1/395

2/395

3/395

A–C

D–F

G–I

99

535

324

254

99

324

99

799

A–D

A–C

A–C

A–C

U.S. V CORPS' BATTLES

393rd and 394th Infantry Regiments

Defence of the Elsenborn Ridge – December 16-17

Elsenborn ridge does not appear on any map of Belgium, being just a name of convenience adopted by the men of Walter Lauer's 99th Infantry Division when they were assigned this sector of the front on 9 November 1944. It is merely an area of high ground between the Rur valley at Monschau and the Losheim gap (another name which does not appear on maps) to the south. Yet it was the spirited defence of this ridge by the completely combat inexperienced men of the 99th which broke the German LXVII Korps' push towards Eupen, and that of I SS-Panzer Korps towards Malmédy.

On 16 December the division was deployed along a 19-mile front between Höfen in the north and Lanzerath in the south, with Lieutenant-Colonel McLernand Butler's III/395th battalion rather out on a limb at Höfen itself because a gap had been created in the 99th's lines through which Major-General Walter Robertson's 2nd Infantry Division could attack the West Wall at Wahlerscheid towards Dreiborn. This assault was opposed by elements of 326 Volks-grenadier Division which itself attacked at Höfen on 16 December with the bulk of its strength. Helped by the fact that most of the 99th's field artillery had been positioned to support Robertson's attack, Butler was able to hold out at Höfen and repulse a succession of costly attacks. The situation further south, however, soon became rather more desperate.

The German artillery barrage before dawn had alerted everyone in the division to the fact that something unusual was happening and then, their path illuminated by searchlights aimed at the clouds, the German infantry loomed out of the mist. The artillery fire did little damage because in their month-long occupation of Elsenborn ridge, Lauer's infantry had dug in well with felled logs and packed earth covering their positions. On the 99th's right flank,

Major Norman Moore's III/394th battalion at Buchholz station repulsed an early morning attack by the 12th Volksgrenadier Division, I SS-Panzer Korps, as did Lieutenant-Colonel Robert Douglas' I/394th on its left flank at Losheimergraben until just after midday when the pressure forced it back a few hundred yards. During this action Sergeant Eddie Dolenc was awarded a posthumous Distinguished Service Cross for singlehandedly covering the retreat of B Company with his machine-gun.

II/394th was not attacked on this day, but the regiment's I & R (intelligence and reconnaissance) platoon was overrun by paratroops of 3 Fallschirm Division at Lanzerath. Then, during the night, so were the two platoons of K Company, III/394th, at Buchholz, and by early morning on the 17th advance elements of Kampfgruppe 'Peiper' overran Honsfeld, to the west of the station, which was defended by a mixed bag of anti-aircraft, anti-tank and cavalry troopers. Further up the road, Büllingen at this time was merely defended by the attached 254th Engineer Combat Battalion and a handful of M10s from the 644th Tank Destroyer Battalion but, to everyone's surprise, Peiper's tanks turned away southwest once they had refuelled from the POL depot just outside the village instead of turning towards Wirtzfeld, which would have rolled up the 99th Infantry Division's flank.

At about the same time the 48th Regiment of 12 Volksgrenadier Division again assaulted the small group of about 50 men from Douglas' I/394th still at Losheimergraben. Organised by 1st Lieutenant Dewey Plankers, the GIs fell back to the customs house on the Belgian-German border and successfully held out until dusk, when the survivors retired to join the rest of the battalion at Mürringen. III/394th on their right had already reassembled there during the afternoon, as had II/394th on their left after being

16/12/1944	18/12	20/12	22/12	24/12	26/12	28/12	30/12	6/1/1945	13/1	20/1	27/1	3/2	7/2
pages 49-61,75-80		81-85	86-87	90-91		88-89							

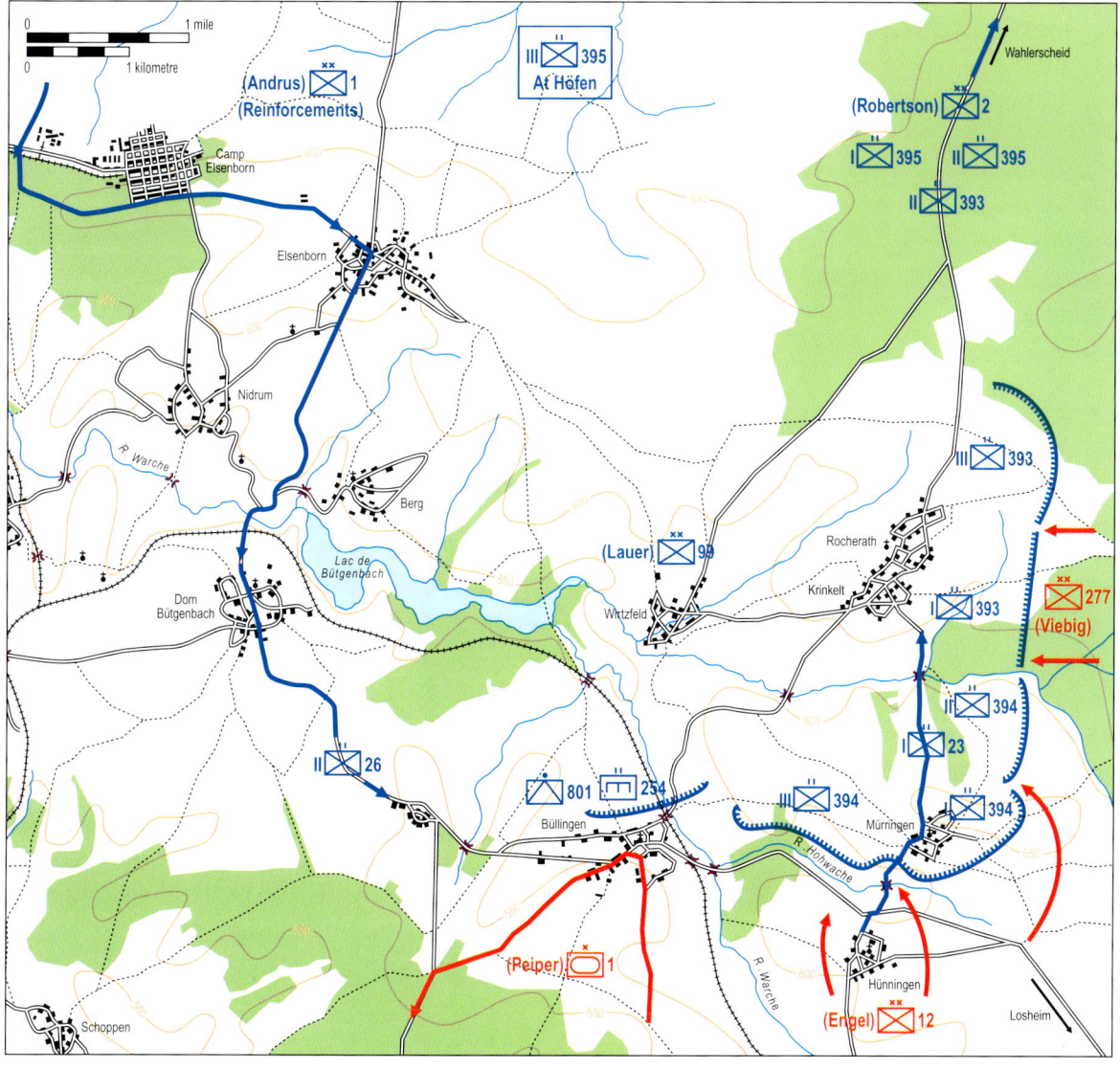

The multiple attacks towards Elsenborn ridge over the first two days of the German offensive severely stretched the inexperienced and insufficiently-trained men of the 99th Infantry Division, but they bought the time needed to win the battle in the north.

outflanked. Meanwhile, Lieutenant-Colonel John Hightower's I/23rd battalion of the 2nd Infantry Division, which had been sent to reinforce the right flank of Colonel Don Riley's 394th Regiment at Hünningen, was in serious trouble, faced by Volksgrenadiers reinforced by a company of PzKpfw IVs from 12 SS-Panzer Division. Hightower wanted to pull back,

but could not unless the 394th conformed to preserve the line. By this time, though, Riley's men were almost out of ammunition and all four battalions now received permission to withdraw towards Krinkelt under cover of darkness.

Here, Lieutenant-Colonel Dean Scott's 393rd Infantry Regiment (less II/393rd which had been attached to the 395th on its left) had been deployed in a two-mile line on the edge of the forest looking out across the German border. Facing them, the villages of Hollerath on their left and Udenbreth on their right were already in the hands of 277 Volksgrenadier Division, which had been ordered to seize the twin

16/12/1944	18/12	20/12	22/12	24/12	26/12	28/12	30/12	6/1/1945	13/1	20/1	27/1	3/2	7/2
pages 49-61,75-80		81-85	86-87		90-91		88-89						

On the northern shoulder of Elsenborn ridge, I/395th helped cover the withdrawal of Robertson's 2nd Infantry Division from Wahlerscheid to reinforce the centre of the front east of Krinkelt and Rocherath. (U.S. Army)

villages of Krinkelt and Rocherath, overrun the American artillery positions on the ridge behind them, and block any counter-attack from the northwest. The Volksgrenadiers' first assault hit Lieutenant-Colonel Jack Allen's III/393rd on the regiment's left flank and by 1000 hrs on 16 December they had broken through K Company and were in the woods to the battalion's rear. On their right, Major Matthew Legler's I/393rd had also been hit hard; C Company was surrounded and B Company all but wiped out, but A Company dug in a couple of hundred yards behind them and doggedly held on.

By the morning of 17 December both battalions were down to about half strength but Allen's III/393rd still attempted to counter-attack. After a firefight with Volksgrenadiers at about 0900 hrs which drove the Germans back, the battalion was then assaulted by a troop of tanks from 12 SS-Panzer Division. Bazooka

fire destroyed one and immobilised another, but the remaining three roamed up and down the battalion's dugouts firing their machine-guns with impunity. At 1030 hrs Allen was told to pull his survivors back to a new line established east of Rocherath by III/23rd battalion of the 2nd Infantry Division, Legler's I/393rd conforming on his right.

Meanwhile, Colonel Alexander Mackenzie's I and II/395 which, together with II/393rd, had been attached to Robertson's 2nd Infantry Division to help in the attack on Wahlerscheid, had so far seen no action. The chain reaction to the German attacks which had started in the south did not reach them until just before midday on the 17th when Mackenzie realised that the 99th Division's 324th Engineer Combat Battalion on his right flank was pulling back to the west. This was under Lauer's orders, but Mackenzie fell under Robertson's command, and an order to conform to the general withdrawal and bring his battalions back towards Rocherath did not arrive until about 1600 hrs. I/395th then deployed either side of the road down which the 2nd Infantry Division was retiring while II/395th and II/393rd dug in facing Wahlerscheid to await events.

16/12/1944	18/12	20/12	22/12	24/12	26/12	28/12	30/12	6/1/1945	13/1	20/1	27/1	3/2	7/2
pages 49-61,75-80		81-85	86-87	90-91		88-89							

U.S. V CORPS' BATTLES

9th, 23rd and 38th Infantry Regiments

Krinkelt-Rocherath – December 17-19

Major-General Walter Robertson, commanding the 2nd Infantry Division, had cause to be worried on 16 December. The three battalions of his leading 9th Regiment under Colonel Chester Hirschfelder were under counter-attack by elements of 326 Volksgrenadier Division at Wahlerscheid; two battalions of Colonel Francis Boos' 38th were similarly engaged; his reserve regiment, Colonel Jay Loveless' 23rd, had already despatched its 1st Battalion (I/23rd) under Lieutenant-Colonel John Hightower to help protect the right flank of the 99th Infantry Division, which was under heavy attack. Robertson's nightmares at the beginning of his division's assault through the West Wall were beginning to come true. He had feared all along that a German counter-attack through the inexperienced 99th to his flank and rear would leave him cut off, and now it seemed to be happening. Fortunately his Corps' commander, Leonard Gerow, was also appreciative of the danger and had told him not to commit the 23rd Regiment and to be prepared to withdraw his other battalions.

While Colonel Philip Ginder organised II/23rd in a defensive perimeter between Wirtzfeld (where Robertson had his command post) and Büllingen, following the scare thrown by the brief appearance of Kampfgruppe 'Peiper', Lieutenant-Colonel Paul Tuttle's III/23rd quickly followed Hightower's I/23rd and dug in east of Rocherath early on 17 December. Hardly had the men of Lieutenant-Colonel Jack Allen's III/393rd (99th Infantry Division) filtered back through Tuttle's ranks to dig in a thousand yards behind, than tanks of 12 SS-Panzer Division overran Tuttle's I Company and decimated K Company; machine-gunner Private Josef Lopez was awarded the Congressional Medal of Honor for covering the survivors' retreat. Two Shermans from the 741st Tank

Battalion were also knocked out, but Tuttle's L Company was relatively unscathed and fell back on Krinkelt. Unfortunately, the success of the German attack had left I/393rd on Tuttle's right completely exposed, and only about 200 men of Major Matthew Legler's battalion made it back to friendly lines early on 18 December.

Meanwhile, Colonel Alexander Mackenzie's I and II/395th, plus their attached II/393rd, pulled back to the north of Rocherath to cover the road along which the 2nd Infantry Division had advanced, and back down which on the 17th it was now ordered to retire. As soon as it arrived, Robertson placed III/38th on the southern edge of Krinkelt. Lieutenant-Colonel Frank Mildren's I/38th followed later in the afternoon of 17 December while Lieutenant-Colonel Bill McKinley's I/9th was sent to block the road through the woods to the east of Rocherath. Lieutenant-Colonel Jack Norris' II/38th covered the withdrawal of the rest of the 2nd Infantry Division from Wahlerscheid, which was complete by nightfall. This complex manoeuvre – disengaging from action, forming column, then redeploying in line – had been accomplished without panic while under heavy enemy artillery fire and is one reason Robertson was awarded the Bronze Star after the battle. But it was accomplished none too soon, because the depleted rifle battalions of the 99th Infantry Division would be unable to hold much longer.

It was snowing at 1930 hrs and the scene around Rocherath and Krinkelt was one of indescribable confusion, with the battalions of Robertson's 2nd still deploying and digging in, and stragglers from Lauer's 99th still filtering back through their lines. No-one took any immediate notice in the darkness, therefore, when three tanks and about 40 infantry passed up the hill through the lines of McKinley's I/9th. Belatedly, someone realised they were German (in fact, it was a

16/12/1944	18/12	20/12	22/12	24/12	26/12	28/12	30/12	6/1/1945	13/1	20/1	27/1	3/2	7/2
pages 46-48,52-61,75-80	81-85	86-87		90-91		88-89							

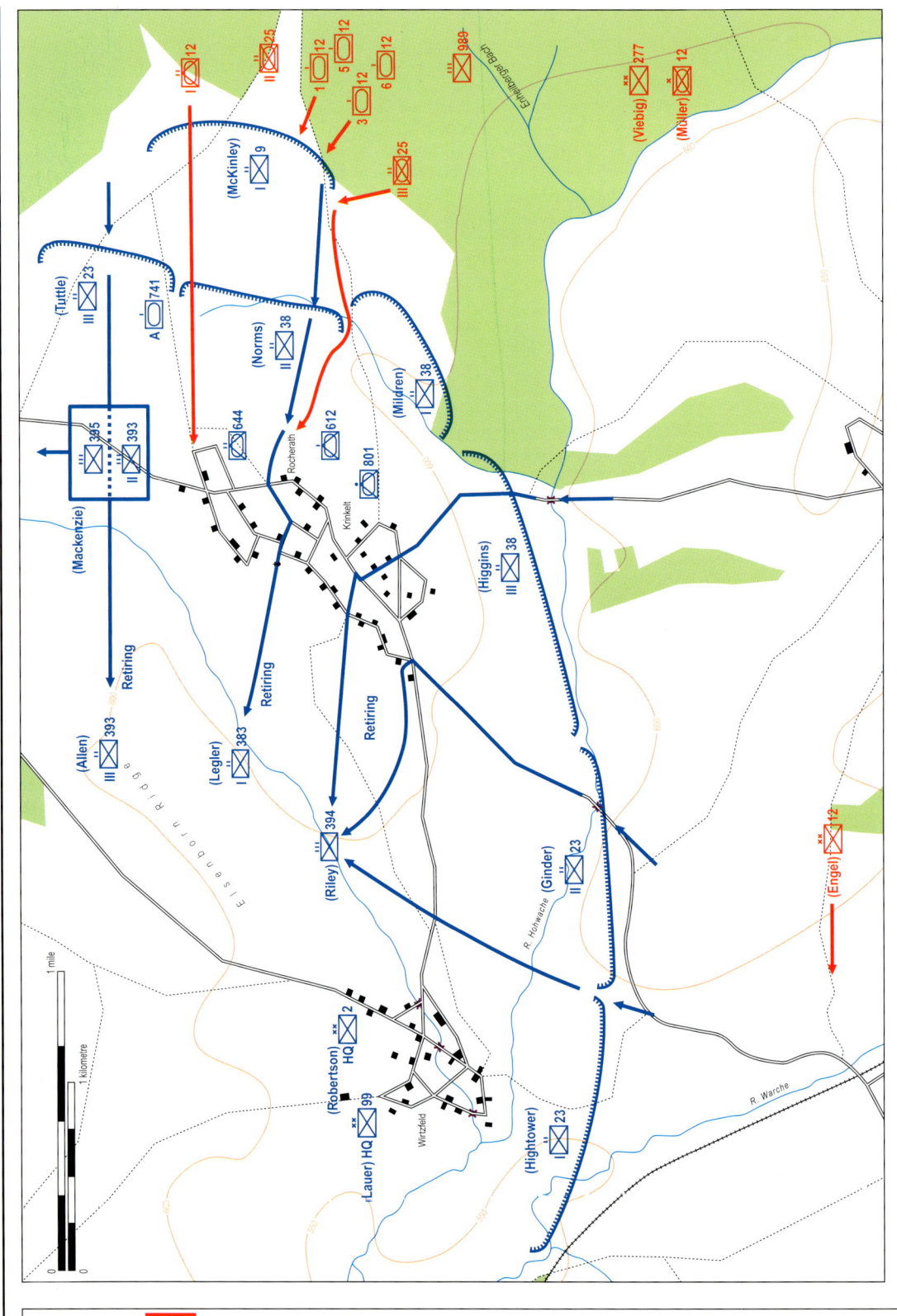

16/12/1944	18/12	20/12	22/12	24/12	26/12	28/12	30/12	6/1/1945	13/1	20/1	27/1	3/2	7/2
pages 46-48,52-61,75-80		81-85	86-87		90-91		88-89						

While the 393rd and 394th Regiments of 99th Infantry Division retired through their lines, Robertson deployed his 2nd Infantry battalions as they arrived.

platoon of Jagdpanzer IV/70s from 1 Kompanie, 12 SS-Panzerjäger Abteilung). Now alerted, McKinley's men gave the next platoons a warm welcome. Two Jagdpanzers hit mines and two more succumbed to bazookas, but five others broke through with accompanying infantry. One was immobilised by a bazooka shot and promptly doused in petrol and set alight but the others continued to cause carnage until McKinley called down artillery fire from the seven field artillery battalions now redeployed on Elsenborn ridge. This broke up the German attack in his sector.

Mildren's I/38th had still been moving south towards Rocherath at dusk, assigned a place in the line on the left of III/38th, when German artillery zeroed in on the column. In the lead, A Company escaped unscathed but the rest of the battalion suffered heavily. As soon as B Company reached the village, it came under

American field artillery was decisive throughout the whole battle. On 17 December alone the guns on Elsenborn ridge fired over 11,500 rounds, breaking up the Volksgrenadier battalions on occasions even before they began their assault. (U.S. Signal Corps)

attack from German tanks which A Company had let through to concentrate on the following infantry, and was rapidly reduced to a single platoon. In Krinkelt, meanwhile, the three Jagdpanzers which had passed unmolested through I/9th's lines were creating havoc, and more and more Germans poured into the village. It was, as the official U.S. History recalls, 'a wild night of fighting' with the battle swaying backwards and forwards, but as day broke on 18 December Robertson's men still controlled the two villages.

Then the enemy struck again, and once more it was McKinley's I/9th which was hit hardest by at least a company of German tanks. Fortunately, some Shermans from the 741st Tank Battalion were at hand to cover their retreat into Rocherath, but there were only 240 survivors. Similarly, in Krinkelt a company of German tanks got as far as Mildren's I/38th command post, but were decimated by M10s of the 644th Tank Destroyer Battalion. Again the villages remained in American hands at the end of the day and, the withdrawal of the 99th Division now complete, Robertson was able to pull his own men back on to Elsenborn ridge during the 19th, leaving just smoking but empty houses for the Germans to occupy.

The German Korps' commander, Hermann Priess, withdrew his armour next day to concentrate on the battle at Dom Bütgenbach.

16/12/1944	18/12	20/12	22/12	24/12	26/12	28/12	30/12	6/1/1945	13/1	20/1	27/1	3/2	7/2
pages 46-48,52-61,75-80	81-85	86-87		90-91		88-89							

U.S. V CORPS' BATTLES

2nd Battalion, 26th Infantry Regiment

Dom Bütgenbach – December 19-22

Since his tanks and tank destroyers had failed to break through at Krinkelt and Rocherath, the commander of the German I SS-Panzer Korps, Hermann Priess, recalled 12 SS-Panzer Division on 19 December to try again, this time on the western flank of Elsenborn ridge from Büllingen through Dom Bütgenbach. Here, the Panzers and accompanying infantry from 12 Volksgrenadier Division were at the time only opposed by Colonel John Seitz's 26th Infantry Regiment from Clift Andrus' 1st Infantry Division, because there were big gaps between the 26th and Colonel Frederick Gibb's 16th Regiment at Waimes and 2nd Infantry Division troops at Wirtzfeld.

Since Seitz was on leave, the 26th's deployment fell to his deputy, Lieutenant-Colonel Edwin Van Sutherland (not to be confused with Colonel Edward Sutherland, who commanded the 119th Regiment, 30th Infantry Division). Sutherland placed the first battalion to arrive, Lieutenant-Colonel Derrill Daniel's II/26th, in a mile-long curve on the ridge in front of the hamlet of Dom Bütgenbach, where they had time to dig in securely and cover their foxholes with logs and sandbags before the assault broke. The battalion had been shattered during the earlier fighting in the Hürtgen Forest and most of its men were inexperienced replacements, while none of Daniel's rifle companies numbered more than 100; however, he did have the support of the 5th and 33rd Field Artillery Battalions behind him, which was to prove invaluable. I/26th was held in reserve at Elsenborn while III/26th was deployed to the left and rear of Daniel's positions, and was barely to be involved in the battle, but five Shermans of the 745th Tank Battalion and four M10s of the 634th Tank Destroyer Battalion, deployed in hull-down positions, would play a significant role.

The first attack against Daniel's position was a

The sudden appearance of Kampfgruppe 'Peiper' at Büllingen on 17 December presented a threat which could not be ignored, even though the Germans did not pursue their advantage. The 372nd Field Artillery Battalion (99th Infantry Division) was just one of the units pulled back here through Wirtzfeld to more dominant positions on Elsenborn ridge.
(U.S. Signal Corps)

16/12/1944	18/12	20/12	22/12	24/12	26/12	28/12	30/12	6/1/1945	13/1	20/1	27/1	3/2	7/2
pages 46-51,55-61,75-80		81-85	86-87		90-91	88-89							

ramshackle affair and deserved to fail. About 20 half-tracks supported by a company of tanks advanced from Büllingen towards the ridge at about 0225 hrs on 19 December. All except three of the tanks bogged down in the soft ground and the infantry were hit by heavy shellfire as they debussed. Three tanks which

The reason why III/26th was not attacked is due to the lake which presented an impassable obstacle, and so II/26th on the ridge between Büllingen and Dom Bütgenbach bore the brunt of the assault by 12 Volksgrenadier and 12 SS-Panzer Divisions. An attack through Wirtzfeld was no longer possible.

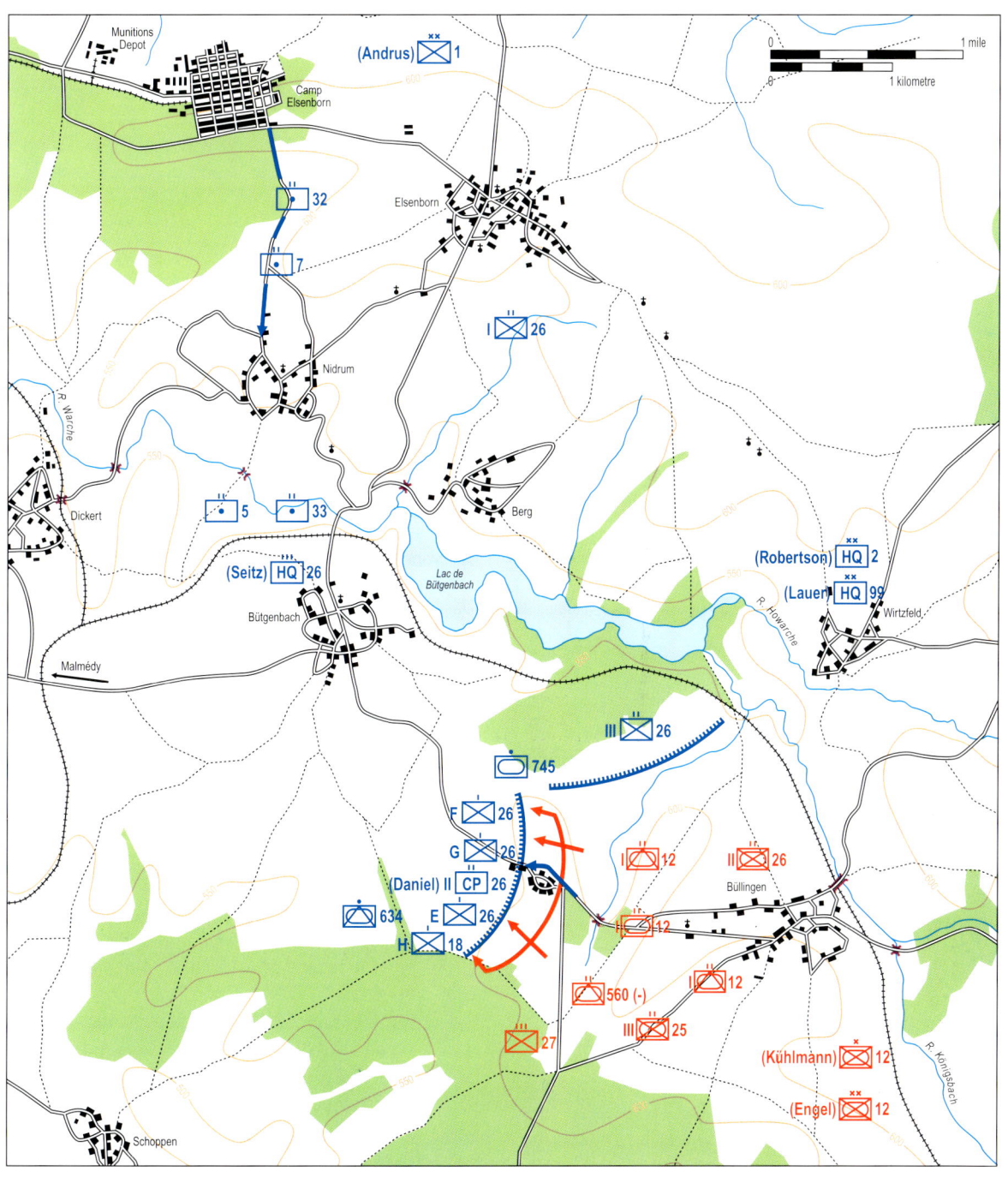

16/12/1944	18/12	20/12	22/12	24/12	26/12	28/12	30/12	6/1/1945	13/1	20/1	27/1	3/2	7/2
pages 46-51,55-61,75-80	81-85	86-87		90-91		88-89							

did reach the ridge were crippled by 155mm shells from the 5th Field Artillery Battalion and, for the moment, that was that.

Daylight brought a second attack at about 1010 hrs. Several companies of German infantry, accompanied by a handful of Panthers, launched uncoordinated assaults at various points in Daniel's line, probing for weak spots. Amazingly, three of the battalion's little 57mm anti-tank guns scored lucky shots on the tanks, and the infantry were again dispersed by accurate fire from all four of the regiment's field artillery battalions, the 7th and 32nd now having arrived. That ended the first day's attacks.

At 0600 hrs on 20 December Kampfgruppe 'Kühlmann' from 12 SS-Panzer Division renewed the attack, reinforced by a company of powerful Jagdpanthers with 88mm guns. Attacking on Daniel's right flank, some of the Jagdpanthers penetrated the lines of H Company (loaned by the 18th Infantry Regiment) and got to within yards of Daniel's CP in the village manor house, but two were holed by concealed 57mm guns which aimed at the flames from their exhausts as they passed; the rest withdrew and their infantry support was again broken up by concentrated artillery

Before the attack, a member of H Company attached to Daniel's command watches alertly from the woods on the battalion's right flank.

(U.S. Signal Corps)

and 81mm mortar fire. Nothing daunted, Kühlmann tried again a couple of hours later, advancing directly up the Büllingen road under cover of the dawn mist. This time the Jagdpanthers were in single file and as they came over the crest in front of F Company, the leading vehicles were hit by accurate fire from the dug-in M10s. Deterred, they swung west to attack G Company, but the field artillery batteries could now see them and, although Daniel's infantry were badly shot up, the Jagdpanthers again turned away. A quarter of an hour later they hit E Company but two were promptly knocked out by bazookas and the remainder withdrew. The second round had gone to the II/26th.

Kühlmann's major assault began next day, 21 December. By this time he had assembled an entire Volks-Artillerie Korps to support the attack, which was preceded by a three-hour barrage. The German commander had also amassed what should have been overwhelming strength: two full Panzergrenadier regiments, all except one company of his surviving Jagdpanthers, plus a battalion of Jagdpanzer IV/70s and a mixed battalion of Panthers and PzKpfw IVs (which had both, admittedly, already suffered heavily fighting in Krinkelt and Rocherath). This time the assault almost succeeded. The artillery barrage, despite intense counter-battery fire from all the guns of 1st, 2nd and 99th Infantry Divisions' field artillery batteries, knocked holes in Daniel's thinly-stretched line. Then the tanks and Jagdpanzers rolled forward with the Panzergrenadiers in long assault lines behind them.

The 26th Infantry Regiment's commander, John Seitz (who had been recalled from leave), called for a box barrage in front of Daniel's position, and the German infantry again faltered and broke, but several tanks and SPGs forced their way through the 2nd Battalion's lines on the right (their left), knocked out the M10s and 57mm anti-tank guns opposing them after losing three of their number, and began systematically machine-gunning the infantry foxholes. Then help arrived: more M10s from the 634th Tank Destroyer Battalion and a section of M36s with 90mm guns from the newly-attached 703rd Tank Destroyer Battalion. Nine of the German AFVs were despatched in quick succession and the remainder broke away, pursued by fire from the M36s. Kühlmann's last attempt, at 1000 hrs on 22 December, again broke through the right of Daniel's line, but was similarly dispersed by tank destroyers and concentrated artillery fire.

16/12/1944	18/12	20/12	22/12	24/12	26/12	28/12	30/12	6/1/1945	13/1	20/1	27/1	3/2	7/2
pages 46-51,55-61,75-80		81-85	86-87		90-91		88-89						

U.S. V CORPS' BATTLES
1st Battalion, 117th Infantry Regiment

Stavelot – December 18-20

On 16 December 1944, in the wake of Omar Bradley's telephone call to Ninth Army asking for 7th Armored Division to be sent to help VIII Corps in the St Vith area, Lieutenant-General Bill Simpson also received a call from his old friend Courtney Hodges explaining that a major German attack seemed to be developing in the First Army sector. The two men had served together in World War 1 and Simpson promptly offered the reserve 30th Infantry Division commanded by Leland Hobbs; the offer was gratefully accepted and shortly afterwards Hobbs himself received a 'phone call from his XIX Corps CO, Major-General Raymond McLain, ordering him to prepare his division to move south. This was dutifully done and the division started driving at 1630 hrs the following day, awaiting orders from V Corps' commander Leonard Gerow when it reached the vicinity of Eupen.

Gerow's original intention had been to use the 30th to reinforce the 99th and 2nd on Elsenborn ridge, but the 1st Infantry Division was already on its way there and, meanwhile, Kampfgruppe 'Peiper' was heading west with a speed which seemed to the Germans a crawl, but to the Americans a sprint. Gerow therefore ordered Hobbs to divert his leading regiment towards Malmédy; this was actually the 119th, but it had bivouacked for the night when the order came, so its execution fell to Colonel Walter Johnson's 117th which was still moving. This continued all night, with I/117th sent towards Stavelot, II/117th placed in the middle and III/117th despatched to Malmédy.

Kampfgruppe 'Peiper' attacked through Stavelot early in the morning of 18 December and headed west towards either Stoumont or Werbomont – which at this time was unknown, although Peiper had actually decided upon Werbomont and only later chose Stoumont after he had been blocked first at Trois Ponts

and then at Habiémont. Lieutenant-Colonel Ernest Frankland, commanding I/117th, was naturally unaware of this as his column approached Stavelot via Francorchamps until he encountered officers of the 526th Armored Infantry Battalion (which had failed to stop Peiper) who told him the enemy was already in Stavelot. What Frankland could smell at the same time was the fuel depot just beyond, which had been set alight by the Belgian Fusiliers guarding it, to stop the Germans using it. Frankland's superior officers, including V Corps' commander Leonard Gerow, expected him to stop and await further orders at this point, but Frankland debussed his men, halted any further burning of the fuel, cleared the jerricans off the road and pressed on past the Fusiliers' fiery roadblock.

The tail end of Peiper's battlegroup was still passing through Stavelot when P-47 Thunderbolts of the 365th Fighter Group intervened (unexpectedly to both sides), strafed the column, knocked out a single Panther, and departed. However, this caused enough confusion in the German ranks that they went to ground on the southern, Amblève, side of the town, allowing Frankland's men to seize the rest. Now, about 1900 hrs, a new German column approached from the direction of Pont: this was actually Kampfgruppe 'Knittel', the reinforced reconnaissance battalion of 1 SS-Panzer Division. A platoon of three Shermans from the 743rd Tank Battalion, another platoon of towed 76mm anti-tank guns from the 823rd Tank Destroyer Battalion, and shellfire from the 118th Field Artillery Battalion, played havoc with Knittel's column, although the larger part managed to get through to the west and meet up with Kampfgruppe 'Peiper' at La Gleize later that night.

The opposition at Stavelot caused Knittel to tell Peiper that the town was in American hands; in fact, by midnight it was, to all intents and purposes, although

16/12/1944	18/12	20/12	22/12	24/12	26/12	28/12	30/12	6/1/1945	13/1	20/1	27/1	3/2	7/2
pages 46-54,58-61,75-80	81-85	86-87		90-91		88-89							

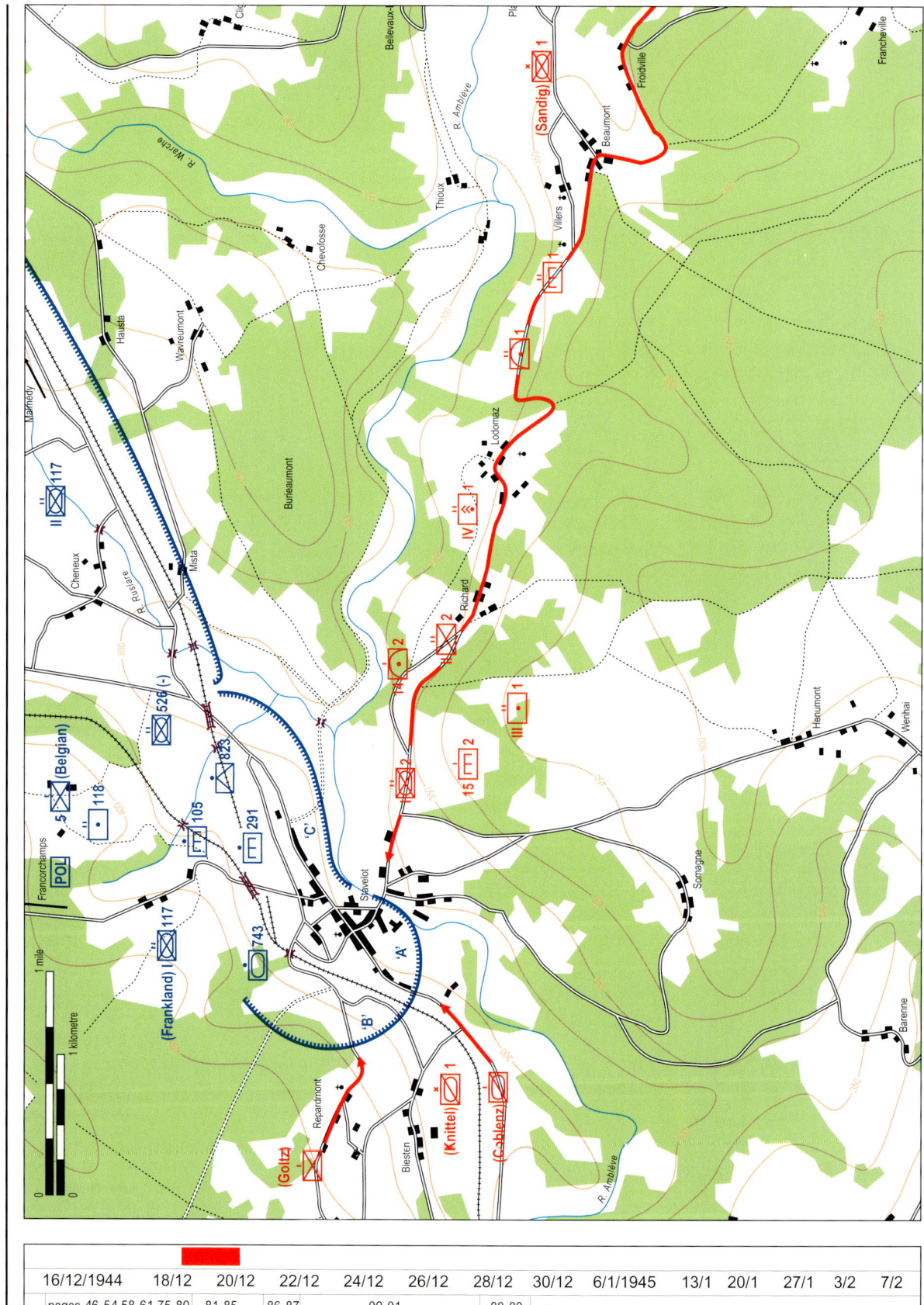

16/12/1944	18/12	20/12	22/12	24/12	26/12	28/12	30/12	6/1/1945	13/1	20/1	27/1	3/2	7/2
pages 46-54,58-61,75-80	81-85		86-87		90-91		88-89						

Frankland's battalion joined elements of other units already in Stavelot to consolidate a strong defence which was sorely needed in the face of the immense opposition from two Leibstandarte kampfgruppen.

three Tiger IIs of the slow-moving 501 schwere SS-Panzer Abteilung caused a scare in the early hours of the morning. However, unable to manoeuvre in the narrow streets once they had crossed the bridge over the Amblève, they all succumbed to well-placed bazooka rounds from 1st Lieutenant Robert Murray's A Company of Frankland's I/117th.

Peiper had fondly imagined that the paratroops of 3 Fallschirm Division which were supposed to be following him would have themselves seized the bridge and occupied Stavelot, his lifeline to his rear, and when he received Knittel's news, promptly ordered him to reverse his column and retake the town. As a result of this, on 19 December Frankland's men found themselves assaulted from two sides: another part of 1 SS-Panzer Division, Kampfgruppe 'Sandig', came in from the east, while Knittel had split his own battle-group into two columns, 'Coblenz' and 'Goltz' (named

GIs of Frankland's I/117th clear the jerricans from the POL depot. The Belgian fusiliers, who had been guarding them, had strewn them across to road to create a fiery roadblock against Peiper. (U.S. Army)

in usual German fashion after their commanders), to counter-attack from the west. The task force assigned to SS-Obersturmführer Coblenz, reinforced by three Panthers lent by Peiper, approached down the road from La Gleize, while that commanded by SS-Obersturmführer Goltz traced a more circuitous path traversing the hills overlooking the Amblève through the hamlets of Ster, Parfondruy and Repardmont, hoping to attack the 117th from the rear. Both attacks misfired thanks, yet again, to accurate American artillery fire. Kampfgruppe 'Sandig' was also thwarted because sappers from the 105th Engineer Combat Battalion, newly-attached to Frankland's small force, finally blew up the stone bridge over the Amblève.

Sandig, however, did have in the tail of his column one of the bridging columns which had been so sorely missed by Peiper, and in the early hours of the morning of 20 December his pioniers waded the icy cold river to begin construction work. Some of them had amphibious Volkswagen 'Schwimmwagen' but, silhouetted against the water, they fell easy prey to Frankland's machine-gunners. Stavelot was firmly and securely in U.S. hands and Kampfgruppe 'Peiper' was now almost totally isolated in La Gleize. Although the Germans continued to press the Amblève line, they were unable to make any further headway or get to Peiper's relief. The battlegroup was finished off by task forces from 3rd Armored Division.

16/12/1944	18/12	20/12	22/12	24/12	26/12	28/12	30/12	6/1/1945	13/1	20/1	27/1	3/2	7/2
pages 46-54,58-61,75-80	81-85	86-87		90-91		88-89							

U.S. V CORPS' BATTLES

1st and 3rd Battalions, 119th Infantry Regiment

Stoumont – December 18-21

Bivouacked outside Eupen during the night of 17-18 December while the 117th Infantry Regiment headed for Malmédy and Stavelot, Colonel Edward M. Sutherland's 119th Regiment got back into its trucks in the morning and headed towards Theux, just north of Spa, where Sutherland had been ordered to report to the commander of the 30th Infantry Division, Major-General Leland Hobbs. Hobbs himself was now at Spa for a meeting with First Army commander Courtney Hodges and the acting CO of XVIII (Airborne) Corps, Major-General James Gavin. Their discussion centred on the probable intentions of Kampfgruppe 'Peiper', now revealed by aerial reconnaissance to be heading west from Stavelot. Would he continue heading directly west through Stoumont, or would he take the more southerly route through Werbomont, threatening the assembly area of Gavin's 82nd Airborne Division which was en route from Reims? Hodges decided to cover both bets with his one remaining reserve, Sutherland's 119th.

When Sutherland met his divisional commander early in the afternoon of the 18th, he was instructed to send his 2nd Battalion to throw up a defence line between Trois Ponts and Werbomont and block Peiper if need be for 24 hours to give the 82nd Airborne time to deploy The other two battalions were to go to Stoumont. Returning to his regiment, Sutherland got his men underway again and split his column when it reached Remouchamps, personally staying with the larger force as it headed for Stoumont. The leading 3rd Battalion commanded by Lieutenant-Colonel Roy Fitzgerald reached the village just after dark, finding to their surprise that a small force of Americans was already there. These were the crews of two 90mm guns from C Battery, 193rd Anti-Aircraft Artillery Battalion, which had been despatched there earlier on the initiative of First Army's anti-aircraft

commander, Colonel Charles Patterson. Fitzgerald urgently got his battalion digging in and deployed his three organic 57mm anti-tank guns and the attached eight 76mm pieces from the 823rd Tank Destroyer Battalion. Since the regiment's cannon company had accompanied II/119th to Werbomont, he was also promised the support of a company of M7 self-propelled 105mm guns from the newly-attached 400th Armored Field Artillery Battalion. While his men were deploying north, south and east of Stoumont, Fitzgerald also despatched patrols towards La Gleize, which reported back that a large force of German infantry and about 40 tanks were bivouacked no more than 2,000 yards away. This was reported to Colonel Sutherland, who had established his command post with the 1st Battalion three miles to the northwest of Stoumont. Sutherland himself relayed the news to General Hobbs, who promised that a company of Shermans from the 743rd Tank Battalion would be with him by dawn.

Peiper attacked through dense fog at 0700 hrs with two columns of Panthers and Tiger IIs supported by long assault lines of Panzergrenadiers. One tank was almost immediately hit at close range by a well-aimed round from one of the 90mm anti-aircraft guns emplaced near a farmhouse east of Stoumont (the other gun had got bogged down in a ditch). Then two of the anti-aircraft gunners grabbed bazookas and despatched two more tanks. Further back, though, the men of the 823rd Tank Destroyer Battalion could hear the German tanks, but could not see anything to fire at. Within minutes, however, they could see all too clearly. Peiper's tanks overran the foxholes of I Company in front of them, causing the infantry to stream back through the gun line. One of the 76mm guns was destroyed by a tank shot, the crew of a second was riddled with smallarms fire, and the

16/12/1944	18/12	20/12	22/12	24/12	26/12	28/12	30/12	6/1/1945	13/1	20/1	27/1	3/2	7/2
pages 46-57,75-80		81-85	86-87	90-91		88-89							

Curious infantry from the 119th Regiment of the 30th Infantry Division examine a Tiger II from 501 schwere SS-Panzer Abteilung which had come to grief on the road to Stoumont. (U.S. Signal Corps)

remaining gunners abandoned their pieces and joined the exodus back towards the schoolhouse in Stoumont where Fitzgerald had his command post.

At about this time, but too late, the ten promised Shermans from the 743rd Tank Battalion, commanded by 1st Lieutenant Walter Macht, arrived from the direction of Targnon to the west. All they could do was cover the retreat of I Company, now joined by K Company which had been threatened with encirclement to the southeast of the village; L Company to the northeast had a direct line of retreat back towards 1st Battalion lines, and laid a smokescreen to cover their withdrawal. As Macht's Shermans fell back slowly in leapfrog fashion, incredibly destroying or crippling six of Peiper's tanks with no loss to themselves, they met up with Captain Donald Fell's C Company from the 1st Battalion which Sutherland had rushed forward to Fitzgerald's aid. The promised battery of M7s from the

400th Armored Field Artillery Battalion had also finally arrived, but could do nothing useful to stop Peiper's tanks, although they shelled the German infantry now in Stoumont. While Macht's tanks and Fell's infantry retired slowly through Targnon towards Stoumont railway station, covering Fitzgerald's retreat, Colonel Sutherland (and General Hobbs, who had joined him in his command post) had been busy organising a second line of defence. A and B Companies of Lieutenant-Colonel Robert Herlong's I/119th had now established a blocking position a thousand yards west of the station at a narrow point in the Amblève valley between the river itself and a steep, wooded bluff. They also, at last, had the support of the division's 197th Field Artillery Battalion, but Hobbs and Sutherland were none too sanguine about their ability to hold. As a result, Hobbs had already contacted General Hodges in Spa and told him that he desperately needed more tanks, wherever they came from.

The only available unit Hodges could think of was Lieutenant-Colonel George Rubel's 740th Tank Battalion, whose men had been waiting since the previous day at nearby Sprimont for their tanks to arrive.

16/12/1944	18/12	20/12	22/12	24/12	26/12	28/12	30/12	6/1/1945	13/1	20/1	27/1	3/2	7/2
pages 46-57,75-80		81-85	86-87	90-91		88-89							

Heavily-burdened men of the 30th Infantry Division slog towards the sound of the guns north of the Amblève.
(U.S. Signal Corps)

Fortunately, Sprimont was a repair depot, but at this time it housed only a motley collection of vehicles, including five amphibious Duplex Drive Shermans. There were also 14 standard M4s, but they had British radios; and a single 90mm M36 tank destroyer. The men of Rubel's C Troop commanded by Captain James Berry worked feverishly with the depot's ordnance maintenance personnel to get the vehicles fuelled and armed. They finally set off early in the afternoon and reached Herlong's battalion shortly before 1600 hrs with the short winter day rapidly drawing to a close.

Meanwhile, Macht's tanks and Fell's infantry company, rapidly running low on ammunition, had been steadily retiring under strong pressure from Peiper's Panzers and grenadiers. Unexpectedly, at a sharp bend in the road west of the station, they came across a solitary 90mm gun from C Battery, 193rd Anti-Aircraft Artillery Battalion. Its commander had abandoned all idea of getting into Stoumont and positioned his gun to cover the road from the east. As Peiper's tanks closed, his gun destroyed two, but then

had to be spiked and abandoned. At this juncture, James Berry's C Troop of what he called his 'bastard tanks' arrived on the scene. Probing cautiously east towards Stoumont station, his leading M4 scored a lucky hit on a Panther, setting it ablaze, but then its gun jammed. The sole M36 following closely behind destroyed a second Panther and, its gun having been feverishly cleared, the Sherman despatched a third. This effectively blocked the road and, with darkness now almost complete, Peiper abandoned his attack.

In point of fact, the kampfgruppe commander had no intention of continuing his assault on the 119th Regiment, because he had discovered a negotiable ford over the Amblève between Targnon and the railway station which would at last give him access to the more open country, better suited to tanks, south of the river. However, he was desperately short of fuel and could advance no further unless the following battlegroups of I SS-Panzer Korps could clear the 117th Infantry Regiment out of Stavelot and reopen his supply line.

Hobbs and Sutherland could not know this, of course, as they prepared for battle on the 20th. By this time, the 82nd Airborne Division had deployed in front of Werbomont, releasing II/119th to rejoin the regiment,

16/12/1944	18/12	20/12	22/12	24/12	26/12	28/12	30/12	6/1/1945	13/1	20/1	27/1	3/2	7/2
pages 46-57,75-80		81-85	86-87	90-91		88-89							

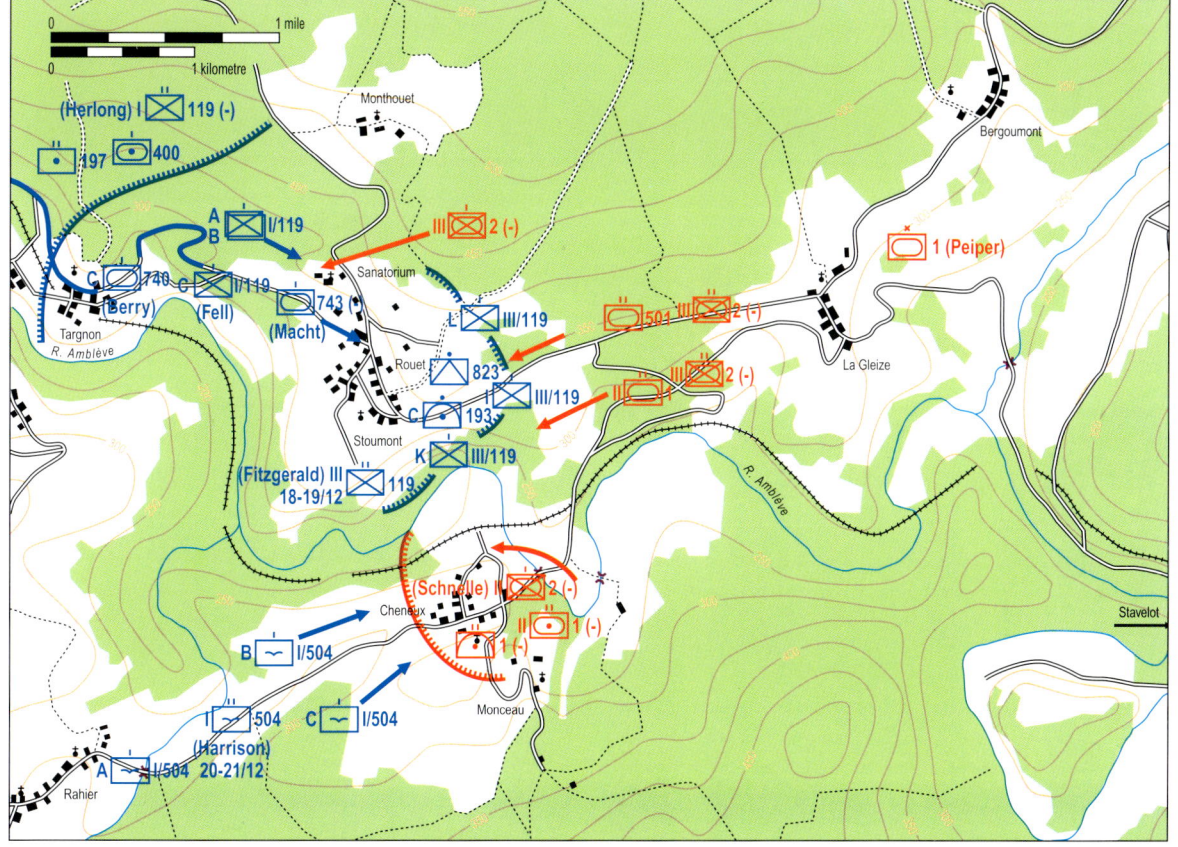

Although Peiper broke through III/119th's lines at Stoumont and repulsed an attack by I/504th at Cheneux, it was the end of the road for his kampfgruppe.

and Brigadier-General Truman E. Boudinot's powerful CCB of 3rd Armored Division was closing in on Kampfgruppe 'Peiper' from the northwest.

Robert Herlong's I/119th probed cautiously forward with Berry's 'bastard' tanks at first light on 20 December. It was foggy again and there was no sign of the enemy in Targnon, but just east of the village a single Panther left as a roadblock opened fire. It did not hit anything and Berry's leading Sherman scored a lucky hit on its gun barrel. Now, however, Herlong and Berry discovered that Peiper's men had been busy during the night, for the road and valley floor were liberally strewn with anti-tank mines; nor was clearing them easy because German infantry lined the bluff on their left. It took I/119th all day to clear the heights and lift the mines before they could continue advancing on Stoumont, at which point

the leading Sherman was disabled by an anti-tank shell.

Herlong decided to advance no further towards Stoumont that night but to finish mopping up on the bluff, which meant capturing the imposing St Edouard Sanatorium high on the steep hillside. He launched two infantry companies into the assault, and quickly captured the building, finding about 250 priests, nuns and civilians hiding in the cellars. Then Peiper's grenadiers counter-attacked and threw Herlong's men out, back to a hedgerow 50 yards to the west, while some of his men forayed out of Stoumont and destroyed three of Berry's tanks with Panzerfausts. Nearly a third of Herlong's men had been killed or wounded in the night's action, which ultimately proved an unnecessary sacrifice because, threatened by three 3rd Armored Division task forces, Peiper was forced to withdraw from Stoumont to La Gleize on the 21st. Stoumont was finally recaptured on the 22nd by II/119th accompanied by tanks of 3rd Armored Division's Task Force 'Harrison'.

16/12/1944	18/12	20/12	22/12	24/12	26/12	28/12	30/12	6/1/1945	13/1	20/1	27/1	3/2	7/2
pages 46-57,75-80		81-85	86-87	90-91		88-89							

U.S. FIRST ARMY

U.S. XVIII (AIRBORNE) CORPS

On the morning of 16 December 1944, Dwight David Eisenhower in his fifty-fourth year was celebrating because he had just learned that he had been promoted to General of the Army and could paint a fifth star on his helmet. He was thus in a buoyant mood for his meeting with Omar Bradley and other senior officers that afternoon, although the subject was a sobering one: lack of manpower. The drive to the West Wall, the battles for Antwerp, Aachen and other towns and cities, had drained Allied resources to the extent that, although there were other

Major-General Matthew B. Ridgway had commanded the 82nd Airborne Division since June 1942 before being appointed Corps' commander in August 1944.

(U.S. Signal Corps)

divisions in England finalising their training, SHAEF had only one reserve to meet any sudden emergency.

That reserve was Major-General Matthew B. Ridgway's XVIII (Airborne) Corps consisting of the 82nd and 101st Airborne Divisions which were currently sitting outside Reims in France recovering from their long ordeal in Holland during and after operation 'Market Garden'. Ridgway himself, in fact, was in England, overseeing the final training of what was intended to become the Corps' third component, Major-General William M. Miley's new 17th Airborne Division. Temporary command of the Corps was therefore vested in Ridgway's very capable deputy, Major-General James M. Gavin, who had risen rapidly since 1943 from commander of the 505th Parachute Infantry Regiment to CO of 82nd Airborne Division.

XVIII CORPS
Major-General James M. Gavin
(pp *Major-General Matthew B. Ridgway*)
Chief of Staff:
Colonel Ralph D. Eaton

---

82 Airborne Division (Gavin)
101 Airborne Division (McAuliffe pp Taylor)
 (to VIII Corps 17 December)
7 Armored Division (Hasbrouck)
 (from VIII Corps 20 December)
30 Infantry Division (Hobbs)
 (from V Corps 21 December)
75 Infantry Division (Prickett)
 (from Ninth Army 23 December)
14 Cavalry Group (Mechanized) (Devine/Duggan):
 18 and 32 Squadrons (Mechanized) (Damon & Ridge)
424 Infantry Regiment (Reid/Perrln)
 (attached 20 December – survivors from
 106 Infantry Division, VIII Corps)
820 Tank Destroyer Battalion (attached to 7 Armored Division
 25 December – survivors from 106 Infantry Division,
 VIII Corps)
79 Field Artillery Group:
 153, 551 and 552 Field Artillery Battalions
179 Field Artillery Group:
 259 and 965 Field Artillery Battalions
211 Field Artillery Group:
 240 and 264 Field Artillery Battalions
254 Field Artillery Battalion
275 Field Artillery Battalion
400 Armored Field Artillery Battalion
460 Parachute Field Artillery Battalion
 (3 Armored Division [Rose] [briefly attached 19-23 December
 en route to VII Corps])
509 Parachute Infantry Battalion (Tomasik) (attached)
551 Parachute Infantry Battalion (Joerg) (attached)

The 101st Airborne Division was similarly under the temporary command of Brigadier-General Anthony C. McAuliffe because its regular CO, Major-General Maxwell B. Taylor, was in Washington.

The two airborne divisions of Eisenhower's SHAEF reserve therefore hardly constituted a force commensurate with his obligations, which stretched from the North Sea coast of Holland to the border with Switzerland. But they *were* all he had.

Reaction to the German onslaught had been, from the most high-ranking officer to the lowliest private, a mixture of professionalism and resolve to resist, or a panic-stricken desire to escape. This is one of the endless fascinations of the battle. Here, a squad of men stood firm and with a single bazooka shot thwarted, or so delayed, the enemy's advance that the result was the same. There, a squad of men abandoned their rifle pits and vanished into the forest. Here, an officer brought up a reserve company or battalion to relieve a threatened sector. There, he abdicated authority and got drunk because he did not know what to do, and making no choice was preferable to making the wrong one which would bring ridicule on his head.

In these various ways the United States' men showed their capabilities and, to their credit, there were in truth few who ran away after the initial panic, inflamed by stories of saboteurs in American uniforms and inflated tales of the Malmédy massacre, had subsided. And into this nightmarish confusion was launched XVIII (Airborne) Corps.

Eisenhower was very reluctant initially to release them from reserve, but Troy Middleton's plight in front of the two important road junctions at Bastogne and St Vith dictated that something had to be done, so Ridgway's paras were let loose to plug the gaps in the lines. Troy Middleton, an experienced field commander and not normally one to panic, could see his 28th and 106th Infantry Divisions withering away. He appealed, through Hodges, to Bradley for help. Perhaps Bradley was partially influenced by the fact that he had once commanded the 28th, but probably not. Whatever, he was sufficiently persuasive that Eisenhower did reluctantly agree to release his two reserve divisions to go to Middleton's aid. Meanwhile, an urgent message had gone to England telling the XVIII Corps' commander, Matthew Ridgway, to get back to Belgium on the first available 'plane. No-one doubted his deputy, Gavin's, ability, but Ridgway was the more experienced of the two men.

The U.S. Official History records that, 'To alert and dispatch the two veteran airborne divisions was a methodical process, although both moved to the front minus some equipment and with less than the

'Slim Jim' Gavin, left, was always a 'snappy' dresser but his leadership as both a regimental and later a divisional commander made his men devoted. (U.S. Signal Corps)

prescribed load of ammunition. This initial deployment in Belgium presents a less ordered picture, blurred by the fact that headquarters' journals fail to square with one another and the memories of the commanders involved are at variance.'

The two divisions of XVIII (Airborne) Corps were at first destined for Bastogne and Houffalize, Bradley relying on Hodges to release forces from V or VII Corps of First Army to reinforce St Vith, and on Patton's Third Army to the south to reinforce and protect that flank. But the threat in the north seemed, at the time, to be the more urgent, so the first of Ridgway's divisions to hit the road, the 82nd, was redeployed to Werbomont to block the Amblève valley against I SS-Panzer Korps. Also attached to the Corps on 21 December were the independent 509th and 551st Parachute Infantry Battalions which had been resting at Epernay and Laon. The other component of the Corps, Maxwell Taylor's 101st, would arrive in the nick of time to secure a perilously weak perimeter around Bastogne.

Meanwhile, XVIII Corps was being reinforced in the usual manner by being assigned units from other corps. First on the scene, actually before the paras of the 82nd Airborne, was Brigadier-General Robert

Hasbrouck's experienced, and well-rested, 7th Armored Division. Hasbrouck's deputy, Bruce Clarke, took over the defence of St Vith from a demoralised and indecisive Alan Jones, who abdicated responsibility. Clarke deployed what were at first meagre forces in a traditional 'horseshoe' defensive perimeter, and awaited results. Meanwhile, Gavin's 82nd Airborne began to deploy to Clarke's west and north, partially to block I SS-Panzer Korps' advance, and partially to provide a secure second line of defence behind which the St Vith garrison could retire if the

pressure eventually proved too much – as it did. A withdrawal would have been inevitable even if Montgomery, given overall command of the northern sector on 20 December, had not issued the order.

The third component of XVIII Corps, Leland Hobbs' 30th Infantry Division, released from Gerow's V Corps' command to that of Ridgway once it had stopped Kampfgruppe 'Peiper' in its tracks at Stoumont and blocked its retreat at Stavelot, would complete the annihilation of the SS battlegroup around La Gleize in

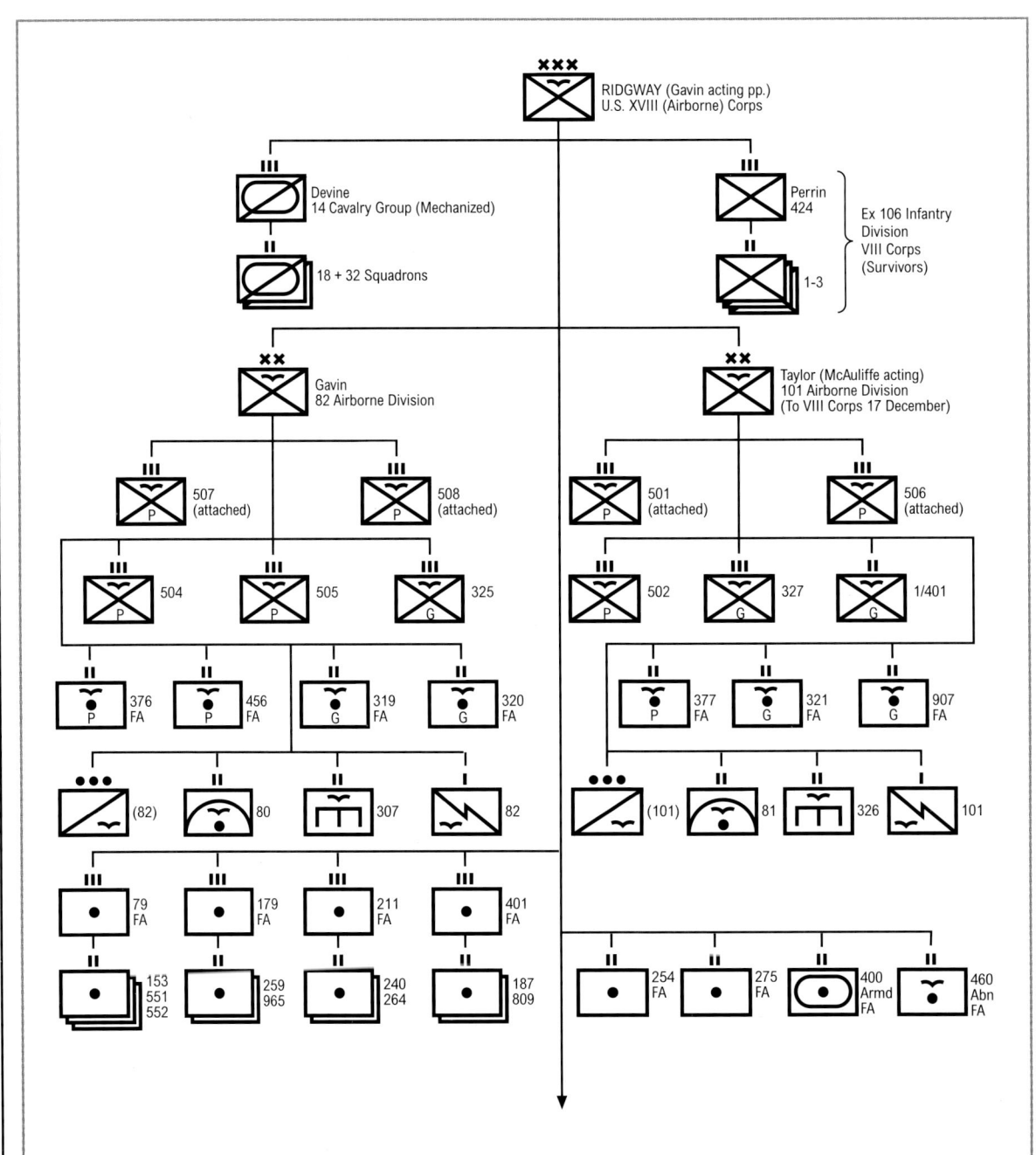

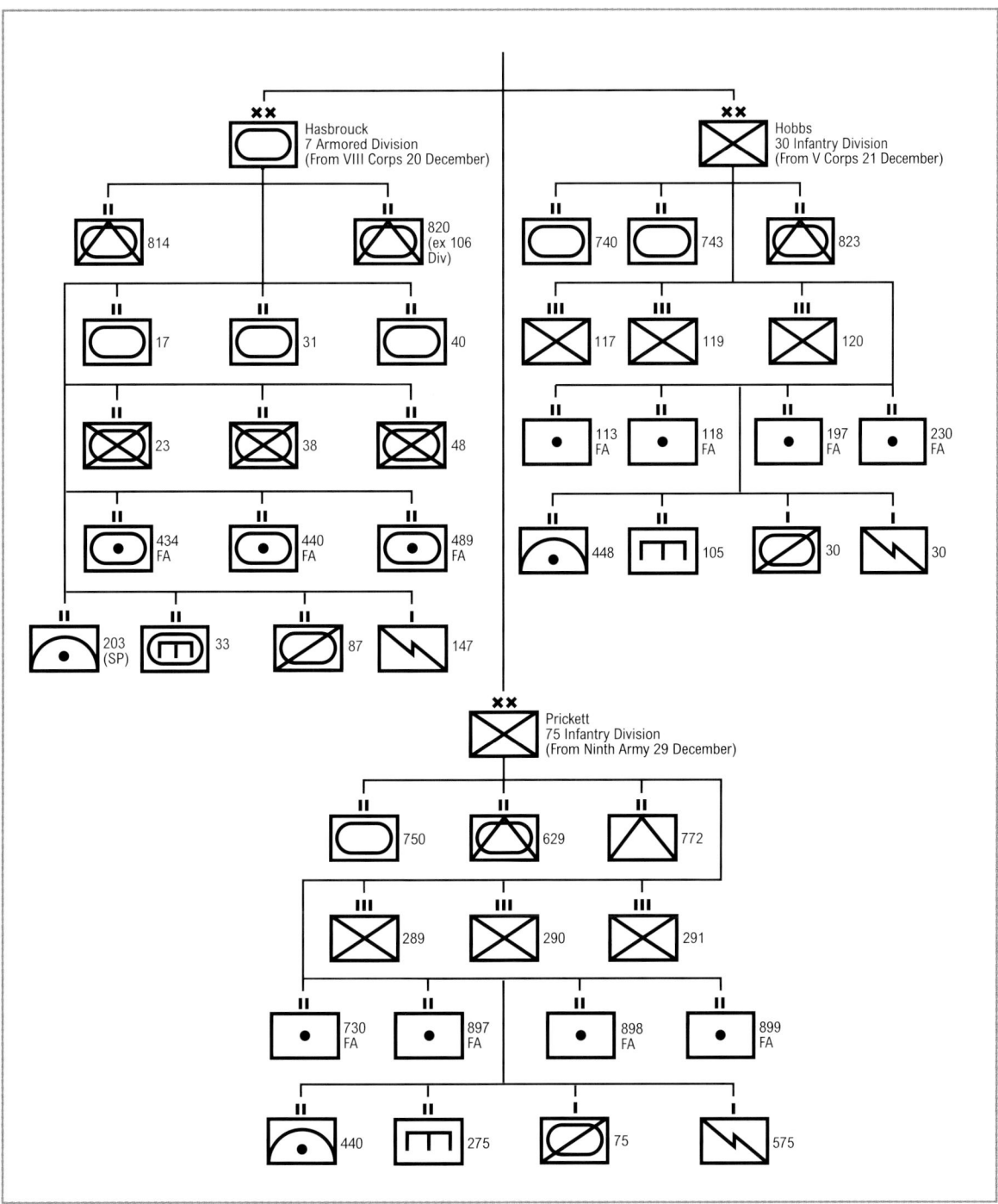

conjunction with the tanks of 3rd Armored Division from Collins' VII Corps.

The last component of the corps, the fresh and untried 75th Infantry Division commanded by Fay Prickett, would enter the line on the south of 82nd Airborne's flank. Between them, they would defeat the last desperate thrust by the remaining strength of two combined SS-Panzer Divisions and, within a month – but an astonishingly long month – wrest St Vith back from the enemy and pursue him behind the West Wall and beyond.

The 82nd and 101st Airborne Divisions themselves were not involved in any further major operations once the Rur had been crossed in force and it was left to the latest addition to XVIII Corps, the 17th Airborne Division, to take the glory of assisting in the assault over the Rhine in March.

82nd Airborne Division 'All American'

The 'All Americans' were in a rest area near Reims, recovering from their stiff battle in Holland, when they were ordered to move into Belgium to help block the German advance. Together with the 101st Airborne, the 82nd comprised the whole of Eisenhower's SHAEF reserve, and it was only with reluctance that he acceded to Hodges' request to release them, relayed to him by Bradley on 17 December. Hodges had already thrown all his own First Army reserves into the battle, and Simpson was

Major-General James M. Gavin had led the 505th Parachute Infantry Regiment on Sicily and in Normandy before being promoted to command of the 82nd.

(U.S. Signal Corps)

82nd AIRBORNE DIVISION
Major-General James M. Gavin
HQ Company

---

504 Parachute Infantry Regiment (Tucker)
505 Parachute Infantry Regiment (Ekman)
325 Glider Infantry Regiment (Billingslea)
376 Parachute Field Artillery Battalion
456 Parachute Field Artillery Battalion
319 Glider Field Artillery Battalion
320 Glider Field Artillery Battalion
80 Airborne Anti-Aircraft Battalion Reconnaissance Platoon
307 Airborne Engineer Battalion
307 Airborne Medical Company
82 Airborne Signals Company
407 Airborne Quartermaster Company
782 Airborne Ordnance Maintenance Company
507 Parachute Infantry Regiment (Raff) (attached)
508 Parachute Infantry Regiment (Lindquist) (attached)
509 Parachute Infantry Battalion (Tomasik) (attached)

---

sending all he could spare from Ninth Army, but Hodges was still worried in particular about the plight of VIII Corps.

The 82nd Airborne had no organic transport but within a matter of hours the local Communications Zone personnel had assembled enough 25- and 10-ton trucks to transport Gavin's 12,000 men and all their equipment towards the front. The 82nd was to take the lead because its men were better rested and better prepared for immediate combat then their companions in the 101st, and Gavin (who was the acting XVIII Corps' commander while Ridgway was in England) wasted no time in hurrying to Hodges' headquarters in Spa, which he reached at lunchtime on the 18th.

At this point no-one had decided exactly where the two airborne divisions were to be deployed. The VIII Corps' commander, Troy Middleton, had asked for them to be sent to Bastogne and Houffalize, relying on Gerow's V Corps to safeguard his northern flank. However, when Gavin arrived at Spa he found the First Army staff more concerned about Kampfgruppe 'Peiper's' westward drive in V Corps' sector than about Bastogne. It was therefore decided to divert the 82nd

to Werbomont, which seemed to be a key town around which to deploy a strong blocking force. Gavin promptly set out for Werbomont, where he established his command post, and leading elements of the division began assembling there as night fell.

Most of the remainder had arrived by the following morning, as had the XVIII Corps' commander, Matthew Ridgway, following a conference with Middleton in Bastogne. Ridgway, with the 101st Airborne now on its way to Bastogne, established his own CP close to Gavin's. The 82nd would, it was decided, initially be deployed in an irregular line stretching from the River Amblève through Manhay and Houffalize to La Roche on the River Ourthe. This would both block Peiper and provide a 'safety net' for Middleton's left flank division, the 106th Infantry, which was under increasing pressure in the Schnee Eifel and would, in fact, be almost completely cut off by the end of the day.

Gavin deployed Colonel Reuben Tucker's 504th Parachute Infantry Regiment northwards towards La Gleize, where it was to establish a blocking position at Rahier, south of Stoumont. To its right, backing the small force of engineers in Trois Ponts, he assigned

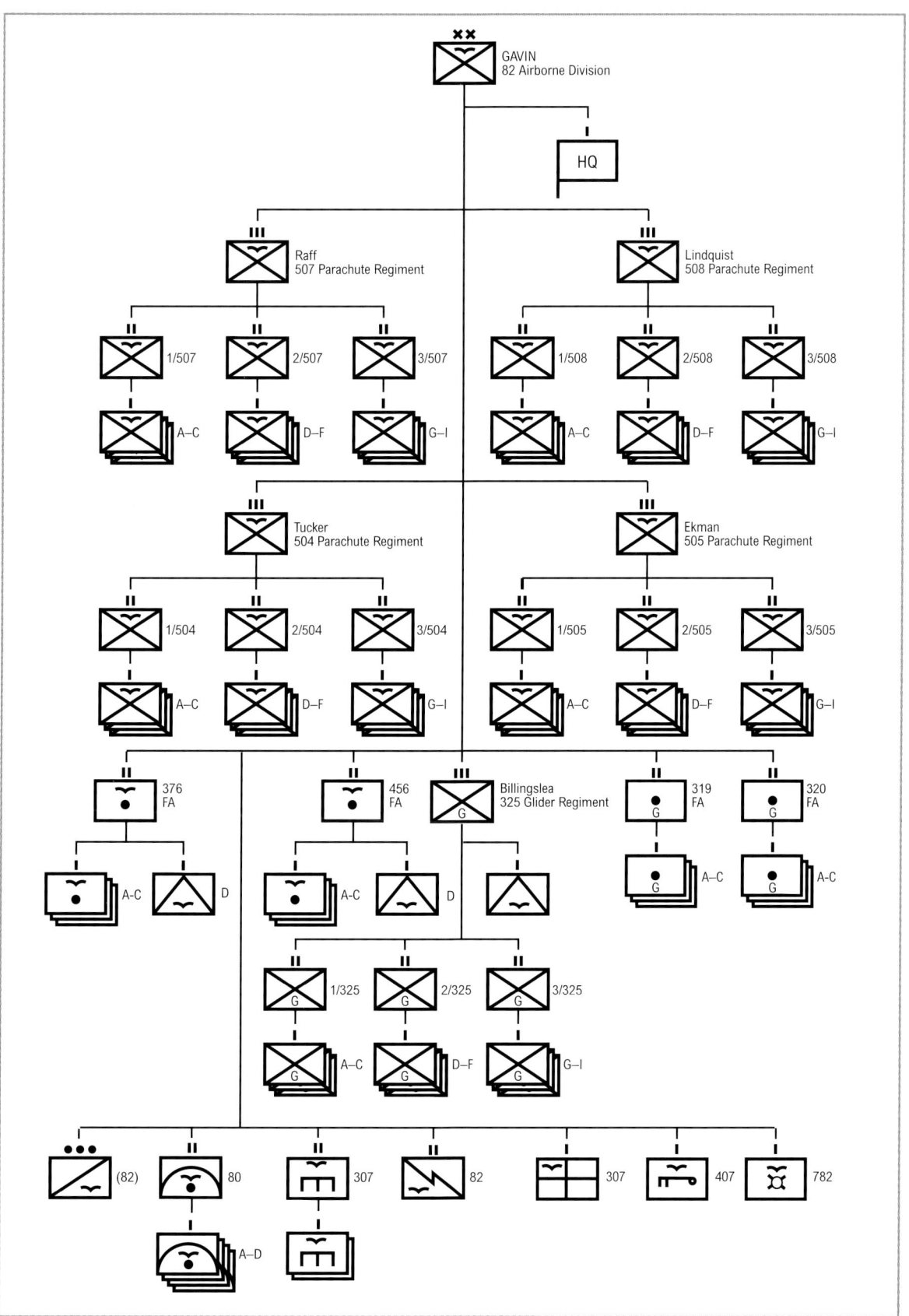

Above: **Men of Colonel Roy Lindquist's 508th Parachute Infantry Regiment at Arbrefontaine.** (U.S. Signal Corps)

Colonel Bill Ekman's 505th which was to base itself around Basse-Bodeux. In support behind them between Chevron and Bra, west of the little steep-banked River Lienne, Gavin put Colonel Roy Lindquist's 508th. The bulk of Colonel Charles Billingslea's 325th Glider Infantry Regiment he kept as a divisional reserve in and around Werbomont, but its 3rd Battalion was sent south towards Hotton. These deployments completed, and satisfied they had done all they could for the moment, Gavin and Ridgway could now only await events.

It was an unusual situation for the men of the 82nd, who were more accustomed to being flown rather than trucked into battle and to being deployed offensively rather than defensively. The original 82nd Division had been disbanded after World War 1 but it was reactivated on 25 March 1942 in the wake of the Japanese attack on Pearl Harbor. Its first commander was none other than Major-General Omar Bradley but his then deputy, Brigadier-General Matthew Ridgway, took over three months later and in August, redesignated 'Airborne', the 82nd began training at Fort Bragg, on the west side of the Hudson River north of New York. In April 1943 the division embarked for Casablanca in North Africa, earmarked for the planned invasion of Sicily in the summer, operation 'Husky'.

Assigned to Bradley's II Corps, the division was dropped inland from Gela in two waves on 9 and 11 July. Unfortunately the drops were badly scattered and several aircraft lost to 'friendly' flak, but the division

fought its way to Trápani on the west coast of the island. Then, at the beginning of September, the 82nd dropped at Salerno to provide badly-needed support for General Mark Clark's Fifth Army and fought its way into Naples on 1 October. Next, while the bulk of the division returned to England to begin training for

Below: **Men of Reuben Tucker's II/504th Parachute Infantry advance through Werbomont towards Rahier. The regiment's 1st Battalion suffered very heavy casualties when it tried to break through Kampfgruppe 'Peiper's' rearguard at Cheneux.** (U.S. Signal Corps)

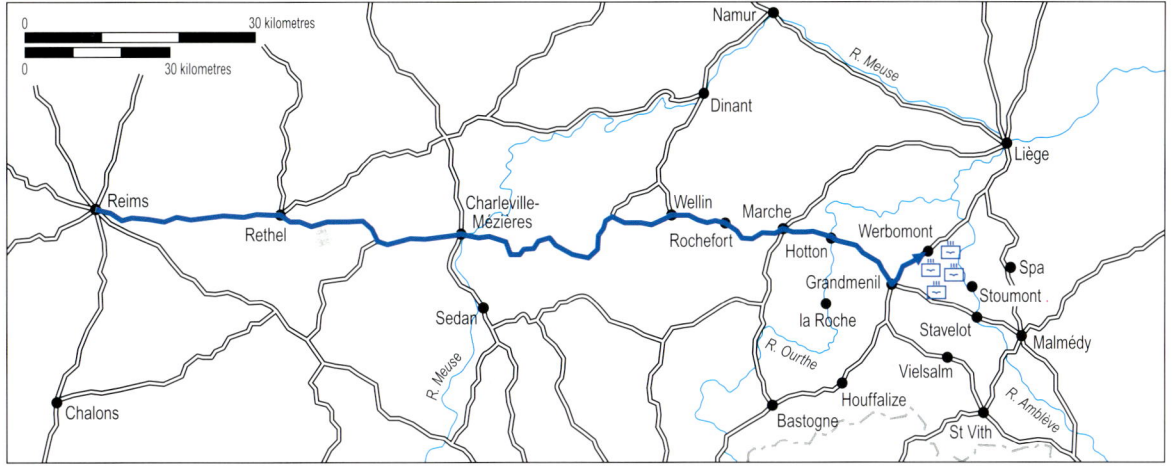

Rushing the 82nd Airborne Division all the way from Reims to Werbomont – over 100 miles along largely sub-standard roads in the middle of winter – was a significant achievement.

D-Day, the 504th stayed behind and landed at Anzio in January 1944.

On 6 June the division was dropped around Ste-Mère-Eglise inland from 'Utah' beach and, despite some tough opposition established blocking positions against counter-attack until the 4th Infantry Division came ashore later in the day. The division remained in Normandy until 13 July when it again returned to England. Its next operation was in September, by which time Ridgway had become XVIII (Airborne) Corps' commmander, Gavin had stepped into his

shoes as CO of the 82nd and Bill Ekman had taken over the 505th Regiment. The division now dropped at Nijmegen to secure bridges over the Waal and Maas-Waal Canal, which it accomplished despite fierce opposition, but operation 'Market Garden' was doomed because the British XXX Corps was unable to reach 1st Airborne Division at Arnhem in time.

After a well-deserved rest, the men of Gavin's 82nd were in fine fettle when they were rushed to Werbomont in December. They held their positions against German attacks across the River Salm, although with the evacuation of St Vith Ridgway had to pull them back from Manhay to shorten his line, even before Montgomery ordered it.

The division began counter-attacking northeast of Bra on 27 December. During this phase of operations, Major Edmund Tomasik's veteran 509th Battalion, which had been attached to the division on the 21st and had already seen extensive action against 2 SS-Panzer Division near Hotton, was heavily involved in the battle for Sadzot. From an initial strength of 745 men there were only 55 survivors, including Tomasik. Like Colonel Wood Joerg's 551st Parachute Infantry Battalion, which had been attached to 30th Infantry Division and similarly mauled at Rochelinval, the battalion was disbanded. By 4 January 1945 the 82nd had reached Salm; four days later they were in Comté and continued east to Herresbach by the end of the month and the West Wall on 2 February. The division was next moved up the west bank of the Rur to the vicinity of Bergstein, crossing over on the 17th before being pulled out of the line. After resting outside Reims (and missing the Rhine crossing which was entrusted to the 17th Airborne Division), the 82nd was assigned security duties in Köln until 25 April. It pushed on to the River Elbe at the end of the month and took the surrender of the German Twenty-First Armee on 2 May.

7th Armored Division
'Lucky Seventh'

Brigadier-General Robert Hasbrouck's 7th Armored Division was in XIII Corps Reserve, Ninth Army, north of Aachen when what the newspapers were to call 'Rundstedt's Offensive' opened on 16 December. Lieutenant-General William Simpson had been intending to use the division – which was well rested, having taken no part in the advance towards the River Rur during November – in Ninth Army's planned operation 'Dagger' across the Rur once the dams had been neutralised. But at SHAEF headquarters, Bradley picked on the 7th as the armoured division which could most quickly be sent to the aid of VIII Corps at St Vith, and Hasbrouck took a telephone call at 1730 hrs on the 16th alerting

7th ARMORED DIVISION
Brigadier-General Robert W. Hasbrouck
HQ Company and HQ Companies,
Combat Commands A, B and R

17 Tank Battalion (Wemple)
31 Tank Battalion (Erlenbusch)
40 Tank Battalion
23 Armored Infantry Battalion (Rhea)
38 Armored Infantry Battalion (Fuller)
48 Armored Infantry Battalion (Rosenbaum)
434 Armored Field Artillery Battalion
440 Armored Field Artillery Battalion
489 Armored Field Artillery Battalion
87 Cavalry Reconnaissance Squadron, Mechanized
33 Armored Engineer Battalion
77 Medical Battalion, Armored
147 Armored Signal Company
129 Armored Ordnance Maintenance Battalion
203 Anti-Aircraft Artillery Auto-Weapons Battalion
  (Self-Propelled) (attached)
814 Tank Destroyer Battalion (attached)
820 Tank Destroyer Battalion (attached 25 December,
  ex 106 Infantry Division)

Brigadier-General Robert W. Hasbrouck conducted a skilful defence of St Vith until ordered to withdraw.
(U.S. Signal Corps)

him to be prepared to move south. Where or why was not specified, but within an astonishing two hours Hasbrouck's division was ready.

Using two routes, one of which twice took CCR south through road junctions which only minutes later would be crossed by Kampfgruppe 'Peiper', neither being aware of the other, the division was expected to begin arriving in St Vith early on the afternoon of 17 December. In fact the 87th Cavalry Reconnaissance Squadron arrived just before 1400 hrs. Brigadier-General Bruce Clarke, commander of CCB, had already arrived by Jeep and the CO of the 106th Infantry Division, Major-General Alan Jones, turned responsibility for the defence of St Vith over to him pending Hasbrouck's own arrival.

As the various elements of 7th Armored arrived, they were deployed in a rough semi-circle north and east of the town with CCR furthest west near Recht, CCA in the centre near Beho and CCB furthest east at

Prümerberg on the Schönberg road. To their east Jones' 106th Infantry Division was already in deep trouble but when Hasbrouck himself arrived at 1600 hrs, he decided against an immediate counter-attack in favour of consolidating an all-round defence. Leaving Clarke in tactical command at St Vith, he established his own headquarters in Vielsalm.

Over the next few days the German LXVI Korps, which had taken the surrender of two of the 106th Infantry's regiments in the Schnee Eifel, made little serious attempt to take St Vith, allowing Clarke time to consolidate his defence. This was reinforced by CCB of 9th Armored Division which Clarke put to the southeast of St Vith; by the 424th Regiment of the 106th Division which had escaped the fate of the 422nd and 423rd; and by the 112th Regiment of the 28th Infantry Division which had retired northwest after the irresistible German onslaught on Skyline Drive. Advance elements of various Panzer formations –

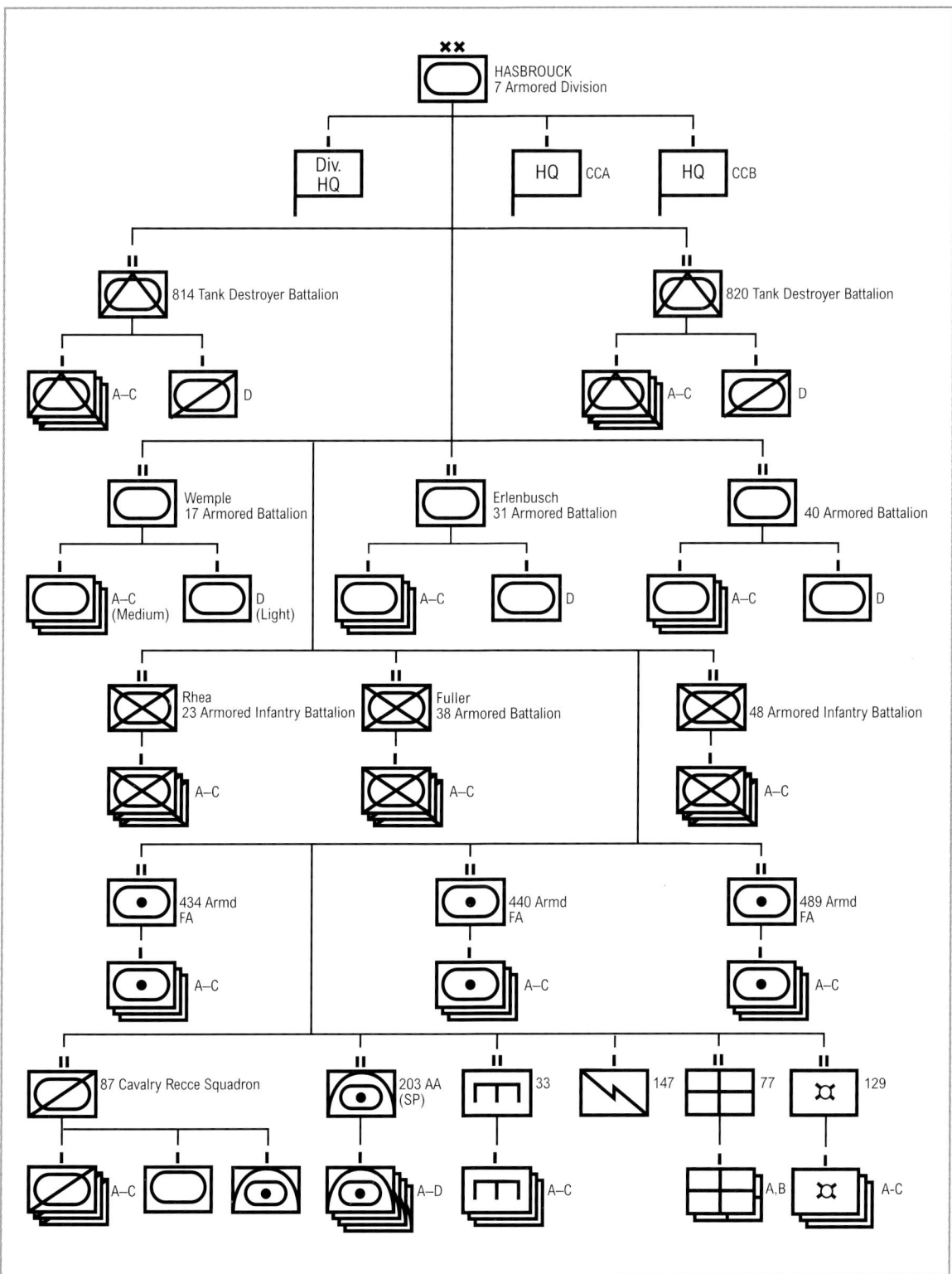

Kampfgruppen 'Hansen' and 'Telkamp' – made probing attacks on the northern perimeter of the defences as they advanced to the west, but were leaving the town to be taken by the following infantry. This was by now traditional Wehrmacht tactics to which Hasbrouck was well accustomed, even though he had taken over command of the 7th Armored only in November.

An artillery tractor tows an M1 8-inch howitzer from Manhay towards St Vith. Weighing some 16 U.S. tons, these weapons were normally deployed at corps level. (U.S. Signal Corps)

The division had been activated on 1 March 1942 at Camp Polk, Louisiana, commanded by Major-General Lindsay McD. Silvester, and sailed for England on 7 June 1944. It landed in France on 11 August and, as part of XX Corps in Patton's Third Army, headed straight for Chartres where it fought and won its first battle over the 15th-17th. The division established a bridgehead over the River Seine at Melun on the 24th then pushed on to Château-Thierry on the Marne three days later and established a bridgehead on the east bank of the Meuse at Verdun on the 31st.

By this time the Allies' rapid advance had outstripped their supply lines and 7th Armored was stranded for four days due to lack of fuel for its tanks. On 6 September it resumed its advance towards the River Mosel and fought its way through to Mondelange. CCA attacked the Metz salient on 12 September while CCB tried to battle its way towards Marigny, but was stopped by a combination of thick mud and very heavy German artillery fire. A similar attack by CCR also failed and the division could only make slow headway towards the River Seille; when CCR entered Sillegny on the 19th it was thrown out with heavy losses. An attempt by both CCA and CCB to bypass this strongpoint and cross the river the next day was again repulsed and the division was pulled out of the line.

It now drove north into Holland and at the end of the month attempted to open a corridor west of the River Maas, capturing Vortum and fighting in the Peel Marshes near Overloon at the beginning of October before being forced again to give up the attack. The 7th Armored, now transferred to Ninth Army, was itself subjected to strong counter-attacks while defending the line of the Canal du Nord and Canal de Deurne and had to give ground west of Venlo and south of Austen. It was at this point, at the end of October, that it moved to Belgium where Hasbrouck took over command and where, of course, the 7th faced yet another counter-attack at St Vith in December. So far the division had not really lived up to its nickname, but the defence of St Vith bought the Allies vital time to respond to the Ardennes offensive, and the 7th's successful fighting evacuation of the St Vith salient back behind the lines of 82nd Airborne and 3rd Armored Divisions was a remarkable achievement.

On Christmas Eve the division was forced to abandon Manhay in the face of 2 SS-Panzer Division and its lines were taken over by the newly-arrived 75th Infantry Division. It was not long before 7th Armored bounced back, though, and on 20 January it began the drive to retake St Vith, attacking through the same deep snow and minefields which had delayed the Germans' own advance. The division recaptured Born on the 21st, Hünningen on the 22nd and St Vith itself on the 23rd, a mere month after it had fallen.

The division crossed the Rur at the beginning of February and was attacking towards Schmidt before being relieved in the line so that its heavy losses could be replaced. At the beginning of March the 7th helped clear the west bank of the Rhine between Bonn and Remagen, where it crossed to the east over 24-25 March. Earlier defeats forgotten, Hasbrouck's division pushed on to the River Dill near Wetzlar, crossed the River Lahn on 28 March between Marburg and Giessen, and established a bridgehead over the Eder on the 31st. The division now took part in the subjugation of the Ruhr pocket, with CCA encountering strong resistance at Niedersfeld on 4 April and CCB battling a determined counter-attack at Gleidorf on the 7th. There was further heavy fighting at Frederburg on the 8th but a week later German resistance in the pocket collapsed.

The division reassembled at Göttingen and drove up the River Elbe to the Baltic, where it met up with Red Army forces west of Klütz on 3 May 1945. Despite the very heavy fighting 7th Armored had been involved in, its casualties were remarkably light: 1,098 killed and 3,811 wounded. Its last commander was Brigadier-General Truman E. Boudinot, CO of 3rd Armored's CCB in the Ardennes.

75th Infantry Division

Major-General Fay Prickett's 75th Infantry Division arrived in France only on 13 December 1944 and had been earmarked for XVI Corps of Ninth Army when it assembled at Yvetot. The German attack on the 16th caused a rapid reappraisal and the division was reassigned first to Collins' VII Corps and then to Ridgway's XVIII (Airborne). The division took up defensive positions behind the River Ourthe on the right flank of the 82nd Airborne on 23 December and its 289th Infantry Regiment faced a fierce battle alongside the paras of Major Edmund Tomasik's 509th Parachute Infantry Regiment which had also just been attached to XVIII (Airborne) Corps. On 27-28 December the 289th and 509th fought a bitter action at Sadzot using virtually just small arms and bazookas against AFVs of elements of both 2 and later 12 SS-Panzer Divisions before recapturing the village after suffering heavy losses.

The 75th had been activated under Major-General Willard S. Paul at Fort Leonard Wood, Missouri, on 15 April 1943 and shipped to England under its new commander, Prickett, in November 1944. The division should have been given time to acclimatise, but instead was thrown straight into the front line, where it acquitted itself well.

After the German offensive had been contained, the 75th went over to counter-attack towards Grandmenil on 5 January 1945. It recaptured Salmchâteau – the scene of Task Force 'Jones' virtual annihilation during the withdrawal from St Vith – ten days later, then Bech and Aldringen before the end of the month. The division was next moved right south to Alsace-Lorraine to join XXI Corps of Seventh Army, 6th Army Group, at the beginning of February. It crossed the Colmar Canal at Andolsheim and reached the Rhine-Rhône Canal on the 6th of the month. Entering Colmar, it reached the Rhine itself next day but on the 11th was taken out of the line and sent north, first to Luneville, and was then attached to the British VIII Corps, relieving the 6th Airborne Division on the River Maas west of Roermond, Holland.

After the battle of Ossenberg over 7-9 March in which the 291st Regiment was heavily engaged, the temporary attachment to VIII Corps ended and the 75th next relieved the veteran 35th Infantry Division, U.S. XVI Corps, between Wesel and Homburg on the

---

75th INFANTRY DIVISION
Major-General Fay B. Prickett
HQ Company

---

289 Infantry Regiment (Smith)
290 Infantry Regiment (Duffner)
291 Infantry Regiment
730 Field Artillery Battalion
897 Field Artillery Battalion
898 Field Artillery Battalion
899 Field Artillery Battalion
75 Reconnaissance Troop, Mechanized
275 Engineer Combat Battalion
375 Medical Battalion
575 Signal Company
75 Quartermaster Company
775 Ordnance Light Maintenance Company
440 Anti-Aircraft Artillery Auto-Weapons Battalion
  (attached 22 December)
750 Tank Battalion (attached 22 December)
629 Tank Destroyer Battalion (attached 24 December)
772 Tank Destroyer Battalion (attached 22 December)

---

west bank of the Rhine. The 290th Regiment took part in 12th Army Group's main assault across the Rhine on 24 March, following the 30th and 79th Infantry Divisions, with the 289th and 291st Regiments following six days later.

Now commanded by Major-General Ray E. Porter, the division was ordered to assist 8th Armored Division which had been pinned down west of the Dortmund-Ems Canal, and the 289th and 290th Regiments reached Datteln on 1 April. Attacking across the canal at Waltrop three days later, the division advanced towards Dortmund in the face of heavy opposition. Reinforced by the 320th Infantry Regiment, the division reached the Ruhr at Witten on 11 April and captured Herdecke on the 14th. After a week's rest, the division first relieved the 8th and then the 5th Infantry Division on 23 April south of the Ruhr and between then and the end of the war on 7 May was assigned occupation duties in Westfalia. Total casualties in the division's short existence were 4,242 killed and wounded.

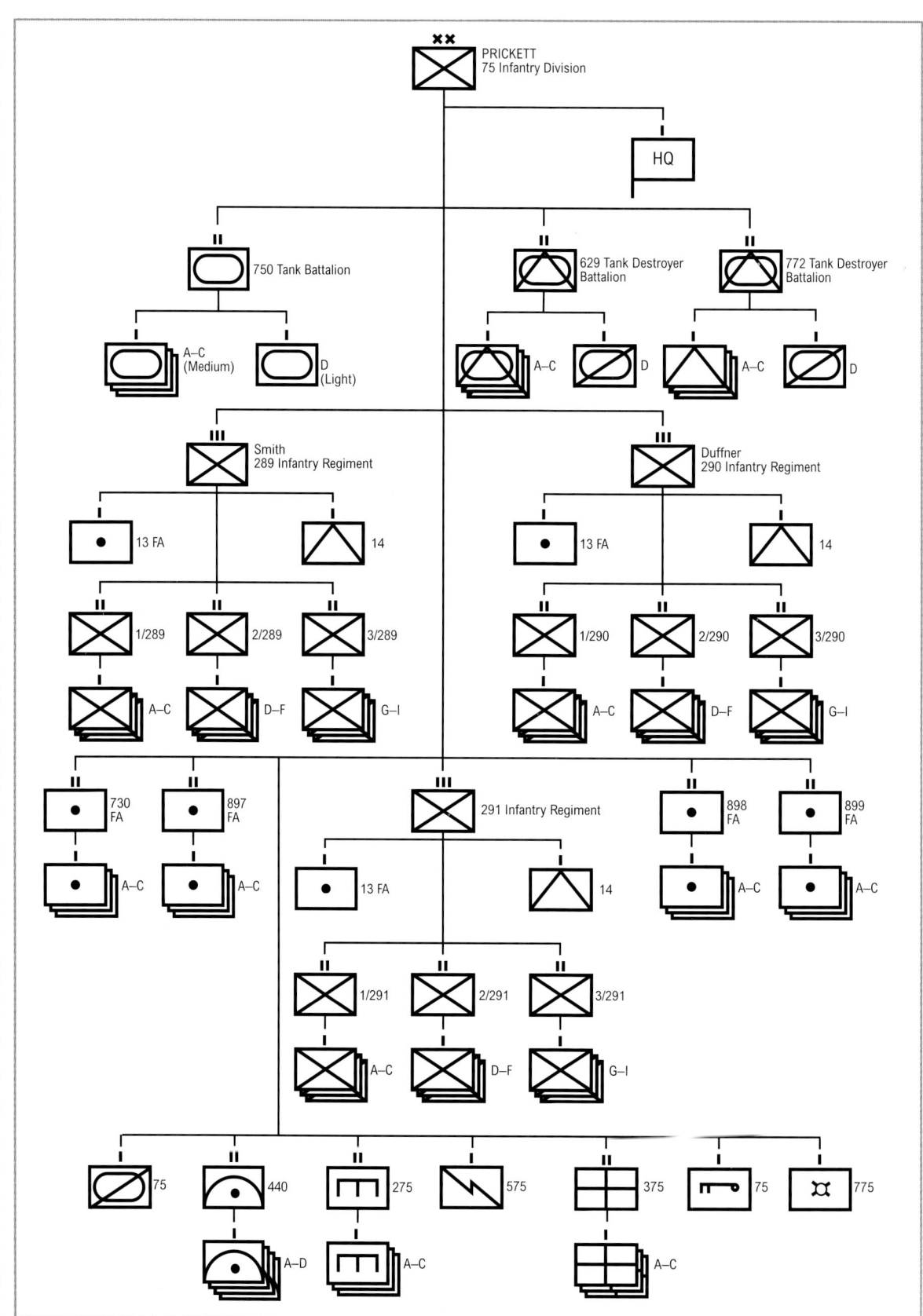

U.S. XVIII CORPS' BATTLES

7th Armored Division

Advance to St Vith – December 17-18

Although not a battle against an enemy, 7th Armored Division's drive to the relief of the 106th Infantry Division at St Vith was a battle against time, the elements and the rugged terrain of the Ardennes and provides a useful yardstick against which to measure the progress of the German Panzer divisions.

When news of the German attacks all along the Ardennes front began to assume serious proportions in the afternoon of 16 December, Bradley's choice of who to send to the assistance of VIII Corps in particular was limited. 3rd Armored Division was closest but that was already committed to the Rur and Urft offensive; next closest was 7th Armored in XIII Corps reserve, which was well rested after a month of inaction. Bradley quickly made up his mind and a telephone call at 1730 hrs alerted Brigadier-General Robert Hasbrouck to the impending move.

The fact that Hasbrouck had his division ready to go within two hours is an astonishing feat which has been overshadowed in the popular imagination by Patton's turning 4th Armored Division through 90° to go to the relief of Bastogne. Both achievements were remarkable but Hasbrouck's actually the more so given the speed with which it was accomplished, when you consider the logistics involved. Having said that, in fairness Hasbrouck did not have any Germans to fight on route to St Vith, whereas Major-General Hugh Gaffey's 4th Armored most certainly did. The story might have been different had one of 7th Armored's columns run into Kampfgruppe 'Peiper', as so very nearly happened.

Logistic planning, in military terms the art and science of moving, quartering and supplying troops, is exactly the same on a far larger scale as preparing for a touring or camping holiday. The car has to be checked, serviced if necessary, and fuelled. Equipment manifestos have to be gone through carefully to make sure everything necessary for the journey and the arrival is complete. Then the route has

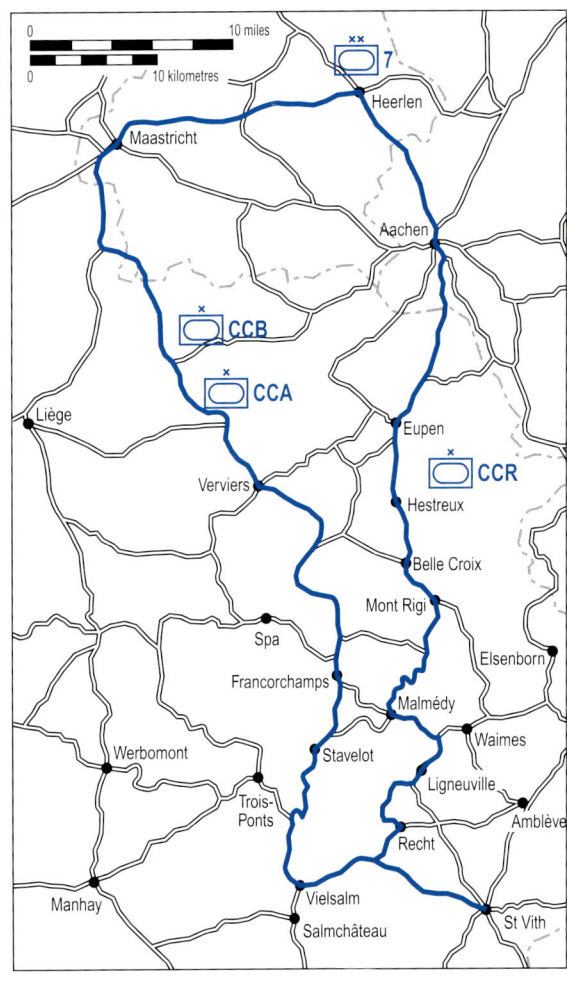

The two routes prepared by First Army staff for the deployment of 7th Armored Division to St Vith.

16/12/1944	18/12	20/12	22/12	24/12	26/12	28/12	30/12	6/1/1945	13/1	20/1	27/1	3/2	7/2
pages 46-61,77-80		81-85	86-87	90-91		88-89							

Robert Hasbrouck (centre), seen with his men after the recapture of St Vith in 1945, was an energetic commander whose leadership here averted what could have been a major German breakthough. (US. Signal Corps)

to be chosen to make the transition as smooth as possible. Now magnify this for an armored division, with, at full strength (which the 7th was to all intents and purposes) 558 officers, 51 warrant officers and 10,001 enlisted men. There are 186 M4 Shermans, 77 M5 Stuarts, 54 M7 GMCs, 469 M3s and 1,061 trucks of assorted size which are not enough on their own to carry everything, so further trucks have to be obtained from the Communication Zone trains. That is the bare minimum for one armored division and excludes the heavier artillery – 155mm, 204mm and 8-inch howitzers – and numerous ancillary services. In fact, First Army moved over 48,000 vehicles to the front over the period 17-26 December.

VIII Corps' commander Troy Middleton had specified that his urgent need was for two Combat Commands so 7th Armored's CCB (Brigadier-General Bruce Clarke) and CCA (Colonel Dwight Rosenbaum) respectively would move first, following a westerly route from Heerlen in Holland, about 15 miles north of Aachen, through Maastricht, Verviers and Stavelot to Vielsalm and thence east to St Vith. Preceded by the 87th Cavalry Reconnaissance Squadron, the whole column stretched for 67 miles and its rate of progress was scheduled at approximately 10mph. The time of departure was set at 0330 hrs on 17 December and the head of the column was expected to reach St Vith at 0700 hrs, but its tail not until 1900 hrs. It was on this basis that VIII Corps' commander Troy Middleton, and the CO of the St Vith defenders, Major-General Alan Jones, anticipated being able to counter-attack in support of the 106th Infantry Division during the afternoon of the 17th.

The column did not actually start moving until an hour late, at 0430 hrs, but the state of the weather and the roads slowed it down so that, even though it made good progress under the circumstances, it did not reach Vielsalm until 1100 hrs – three hours behind schedule. Further delays then slowed CCB even further, caused by the westward flow of corps' artillery which had been ordered to the rear as a necessary precaution against a quick German breakthrough. The leading elements of Lieutenant-Colonel Vincent Boylan's 87th Cavalry Reconnaissance Squadron

(temporarily commanded by Major Charles Cannon) did not actually reach St Vith until nearly 1400 hrs. They were urgently needed by this time because the enemy was probing at the Prümerberg heights only a mile east of the town, and the planned counter-attack would have to wait until the following day. Hasbrouck himself did not reach St Vith until 1600 hrs, having taken five hours to travel the few miles from Vielsalm.

CCR (Colonel John Ryan) meanwhile, took a more easterly route through Aachen, Eupen, Malmédy and Recht, followed by the division's three armored field artillery battalions (which had to be pulled out of the front line west of Jülich where they were operating in support of 2nd Armored Division) and the 203rd Anti-Aircraft Battalion. This column, which itself stretched for 47 miles, did not set out for St Vith until 0800 hrs. Its head was expected to reach the town at about 1100 hrs and its tail at around 1700 hrs, but again there were severe delays. CCR got through Malmédy all right, but by the time the artillery reached the town it was under enemy fire, and the gunners had to detour via Stavelot and Verviers, not reaching Vielsalm until the afternoon of 18 December.

16/12/1944	18/12	20/12	22/12	24/12	26/12	28/12	30/12	6/1/1945	13/1	20/1	27/1	3/2	7/2
pages 46-61,77-80		81-85	86-87	90-91		88-89							

U.S. XVIII CORPS' BATTLES
CCR, 7th Armored Division, and 14th Cavalry Group

Recht-Poteau – December 17-18

As a result of his column's detour through Stavelot, Lieutenant-Colonel Fred M. Warren was unable to open the command post of CCR in Recht until mid-afternoon on 17 December. Warren was, at this time, only the Combat Command's acting commander because Colonel John Ryan had that same day assumed the position of Brigadier-General Robert Hasbrouck's divisional chief of staff since the regular incumbent, Colonel Church Matthews, was missing. (It was later found that he had encountered part of Kampfgruppe 'Peiper' driving west from Ligneuville and had been killed near Pont.) Nor did Warren have a full CCR to command, just the 54 Shermans of Lieutenant-Colonel John Wemple's 17th Tank Battalion because its other major component, Lieutenant-Colonel William Fuller's 38th Armored Infantry Battalion, had been attached to CCB to the east of St Vith, while all the division's artillery was held up in the flow of traffic heading west.

Wemple's tanks were assembled to the southeast of Recht at Eekelsborn, and the only other Allied troops in the immediate vicinity were some of the 18th Squadron of Colonel Mark Devine's 14th Cavalry Group at Poteau to the southwest, on the Vielsalm road. The lightly-armed and armoured cavalry had withdrawn rather rapidly through the Losheim gap in the face of the German threat and had failed to maintain communications between Gerow's V Corps in the north and Middleton's VIII Corps to the south, for which Devine was censured. Now, on 17 December, with no sign of 7th Armored Division, Devine had suggested to Major-General Alan Jones, CO of the 106th Infantry Division defending the Schnee Eifel east of St Vith, that he establish 'a final delaying position' to the north of the little town. Jones had agreed if for no other reason than that Devine's cavalry might be able to buy time for 7th Armored Division to arrive.

What actually happened was that, every time Devine established a blocking position, Jagdpanzers and Panzergrenadiers of Kampfgruppe 'Hansen', the southernmost battlegroup of I SS-Panzer Korps, loomed out of the snow-covered woods and forced him to pull back further west. Thus, in between flitting to and from St Vith to confer anxiously with Jones, Devine eventually ended up in Poteau, a little cluster of houses, totally insignificant apart from the fact that they lay just southwest of a natural bottleneck on the Recht-Vielsalm road which would funnel any German attempt to get into St Vith by the back door.

Fred Warren knew none of this when he established his CCR command post in Recht; he just knew he was here to guard the same back door, protecting the rear of CCA and CCB closer to St Vith. When a Jeep driver told him that Germans had captured Ligneuville, only three miles away, Warren hastened to confer with Hasbrouck in St Vith, who simply told him to hold the village 'as long as possible'. When Warren appealed for some infantry to protect the tanks, he was told that none was available, and when he returned to Recht all he could gather was three reconnaissance teams from the 32nd Cavalry Squadron to reinforce his headquarters' company and the single company of Shermans left in the village.

Warren's worst fears were realised at 0200 hrs on 18 December when Hansen's SS-Panzergrenadiers, firing flares and carrying Panzerfausts, burst out of the woods and attacked his small force. Warren's HQ Company infantry tried to prevent their getting too close (the Panzerfaust had a range of only 50 yards) and the Shermans sprayed the edge of the forest with machine-gun fire, but within 45 minutes Warren realised he was going to lose his whole command unless he withdrew. He therefore sent the surviving tanks to rejoin the rest of the battalion at Eekelsborn

16/12/1944		18/12	20/12	22/12	24/12	26/12	28/12	30/12	6/1/1945	13/1	20/1	27/1	3/2	7/2
pages 46-61,75-76,79-80		81-85	86-87		90-91		88-89							

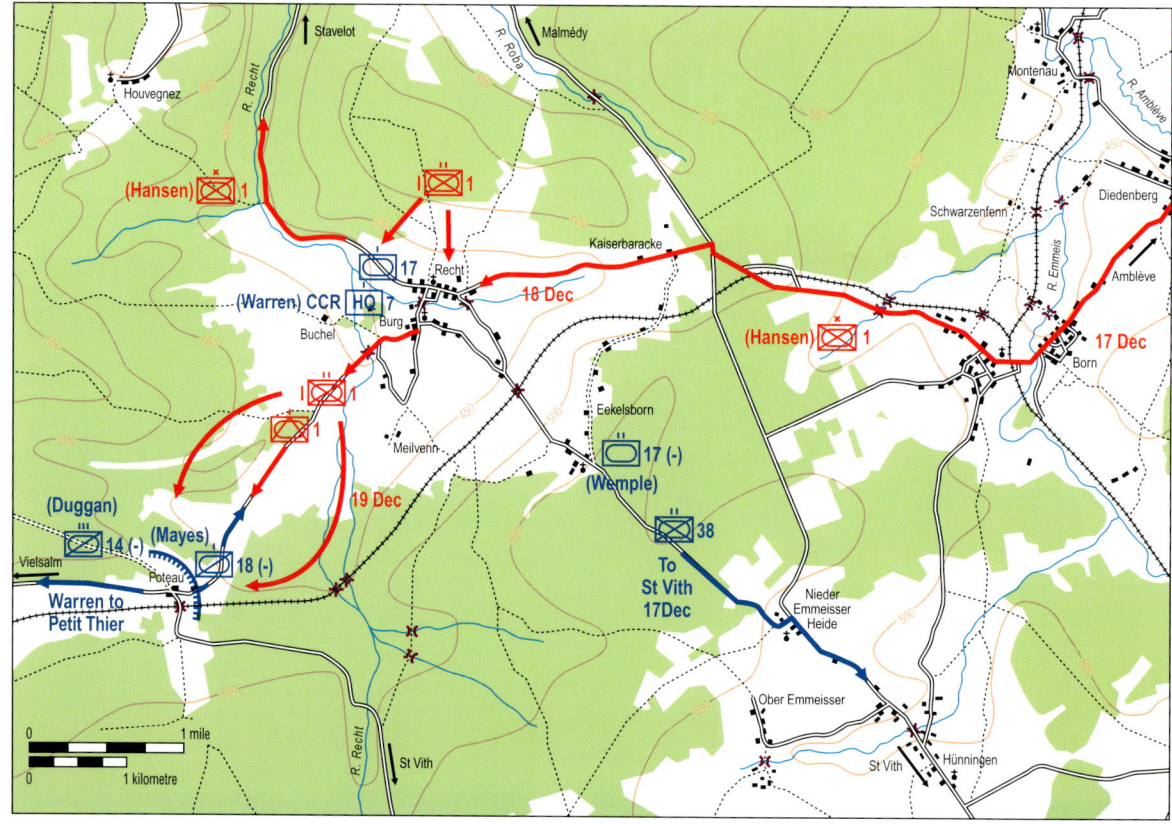

Attacked at Recht by SS-Panzergrenadiers during the night of 18/19 December, Warren withdrew his company of M4s to rejoin the rest of the battalion.

and took the remainder of his detachment southwest down the road to Poteau.

Here, he found that Colonel Devine, unnerved by an encounter with a German patrol earlier that night, had gone to bed and left his executive officer, Lieutenant-Colonel Augustine Duggan, in charge. General Jones, unaware of the true situation on his northern flank, had ordered Devine to take his force back to Born, which they had evacuated earlier on the 17th, and to Warren's amazement, Duggan was preparing to counter-attack in that direction. Warning him of the danger, Warren continued southwest to Petit Thier, where he found and took command of a scratch force of infantry with four tanks and two tank destroyers which had become separated from their parent units but were determined to stop any Germans breaking through to Vielsalm.

Undeterred by Warren's warning, back at Poteau

Duggan organised a small task force of the 18th Cavalry Squadron under Major James Mayes to head back up the road to Born. This set off at 0700 hrs but had gone only a couple of hundred yards when one of the leading vehicles was hit by a Panzerfaust and the column came under fire from Jagdpanzers which quickly despatched three others. Prudently, Mayes turned the rest round and returned to Poteau. Here, the energetic Duggan had organised a line of defence in front of the hamlet with a cavalry outpost on the hill to the north, and for the rest of the morning held firm against a succession of attacks. By midday, though, Hansen's grenadiers were pressing too close for comfort but, fortuitously, back in Petit Thier radio contact had been established with the 440th Armored Field Artillery Battalion. Two observers directed their fire from the church steeple, and under this screen Duggan was able to evacuate his wounded and retire from Poteau. Later in the day the village was retaken by the 48th Infantry Regiment from 7th Armored Division's CCA and Vielsalm was safe, which it would not have been without Warren's and Duggan's efforts.

16/12/1944	18/12	20/12	22/12	24/12	26/12	28/12	30/12	6/1/1945	13/1	20/1	27/1	3/2	7/2
pages 46-61,75-76,79-80	81-85	86-87		90-91		88-89							

U.S. XVIII CORPS' BATTLES

CCB, 7th Armored Division

Prümerberg – December 17-19

At 1030 hrs on 17 December, still anxiously awaiting the arrival of 7th Armored Division even though CCB of 9th Armored Division had already been attached to his command, Major-General Alan Jones received the first reports that German patrols, having bypassed his 106th Infantry Division in the Schnee Eifel, were approaching St Vith from the east. His Corps' commander, Troy Middleton, told him he could use Lieutenant-Colonel William Nungesser's 168th Engineer Combat Battalion from Corps reserve to block them until Hasbrouck's division arrived. Jones sent Nungesser and his half-strength battalion east along the Schönberg road with orders to deploy at Heuem, resting their right flank on the River Our. However when he reached the village Nungesser found the cavalry detachment there already pulling out in the face of the 18th Volksgrenadier Division's assault. A little further back, though, there was another natural defence line on the Prümerberg heights just over a mile east of St Vith. Here, Nungesser was joined by a small force from the 106th Infantry Division's own 81st Engineer Combat Battalion under Lieutenant-Colonel Thomas Riggs, who assumed command. Fortunately, Riggs had also gathered together ten 155mm howitzers from the 592nd Field Artillery Battalion and a platoon of three 76mm anti-tank guns from the 820th Tank Destroyer Battalion. With this small force of some 300 men, Riggs and Nungesser dug in to await events.

Meanwhile, the commander of 7th Armored's CCB, Brigadier-General Bruce Clarke, had arrived in St Vith and the point of CCB itself was only a dozen miles away at Vielsalm, but its route was blocked by the streams of VIII Corps artillery battalions which had been ordered to pull back. Jones handed over command of the defence of St Vith to Clarke, and when the first elements of 7th Armored Division arrived at about

1400 hrs, Lieutenant-Colonel Vincent Boylan's 87th Cavalry Reconnaissance Squadron, Clarke ordered B Troop to reinforce Riggs while the remainder of the squadron was to screen the area to the northeast in the direction of Wallerode. By the time the cavalrymen joined Riggs, they found he had already been in action and destroyed two out of three German assault guns which had been probing the defences.

The Prümerberg defences took firmer shape as the afternoon wore on; first a company from CCB's 23rd Armored Infantry Battalion, then two companies of CCR's 38th Armored Infantry Battalion which had been attached to Clarke's command (the third company was still back in Vielsalm, unknown to the defenders at Recht and Poteau, to whom it could have lent considerable help). The CO of the 38th, Lieutenant-Colonel William Fuller, was now given command on the Prümerberg heights, and pushed the defence line further north and south to block any outflanking move either side of the road. Hasbrouck had planned to counter-attack towards Schönberg on the 18th to relieve the 106th Infantry Division but finally decided against it in favour of establishing a strong defensive perimeter into which the survivors could fall back.

The 18th Volksgrenadier Division made no further attempt at Prümerberg on the 17th, but early on the morning of the 18th a battalion of the 294th Regiment tried a half-hearted assault which was repelled with ease. (The bulk of this division was still engaged in the encirclement of the 106th Infantry Division in the Schnee Eifel.) Later, just before midday, the 294th Regiment tried again, this time preceded by a creeping artillery barrage from guns emplaced just outside Schönberg. This caused a number of casualties amongst Fuller's men but they met the grenadiers with a hail of machine-gun and small-arms fire and 155mm shells from the ten guns of the 592nd Field Artillery

16/12/1944	18/12	20/12	22/12	24/12	26/12	28/12	30/12	6/1/1945	13/1	20/1	27/1	3/2	7/2
pages 46-61,75-78		81-85	86-87	90-91		88-89							

79

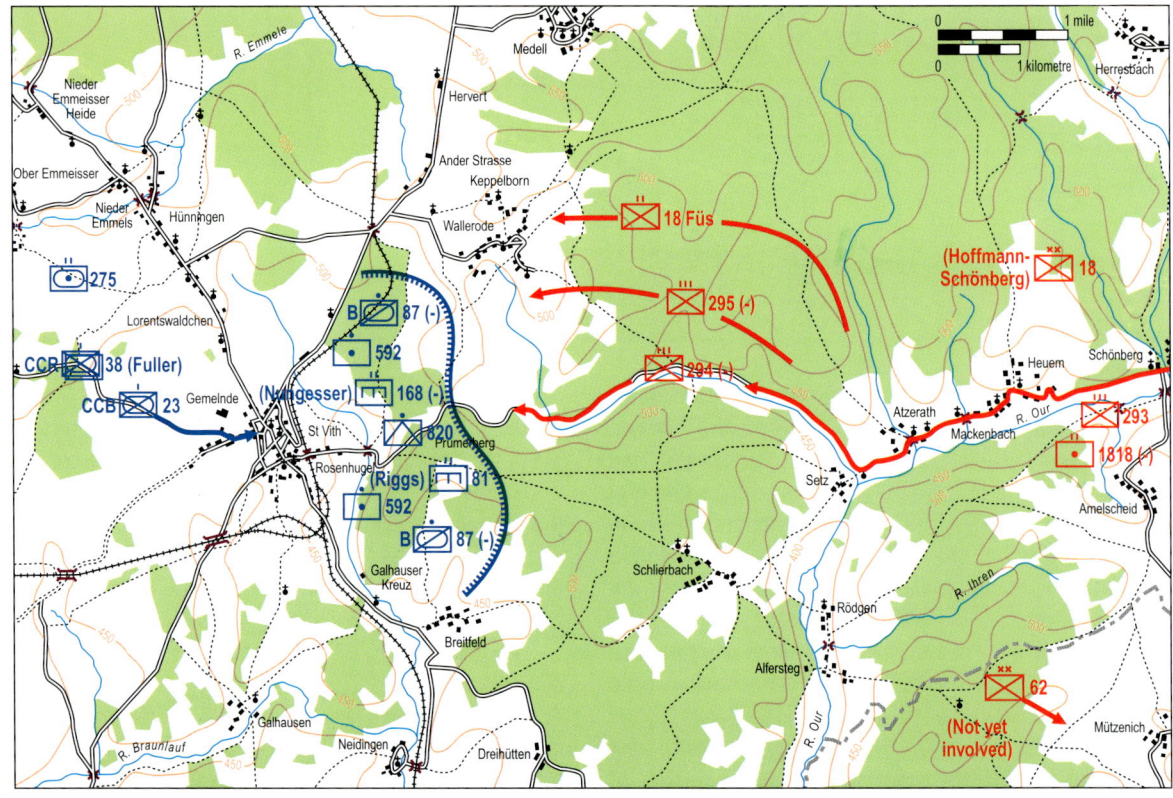

Fuller's task force on the Prümerberg heights managed to hold off 18 Volksgrenadier Division until 21 December when it was finally overrun.

Battalion to the rear of the position. The whole of the 275th Armored Field Artillery with 105mm M7s deployed to the northwest of St Vith also added their weight to the barrage; it was neither the first nor the last time during the 'battle of the bulge' that U.S. artillery was decisive in breaking up German attacks. The Volksgrenadiers' third assault late in the afternoon did succeed in over-running the three dug-in 76mm anti-tank guns, whose crews had to abandon them, but did not break Fuller's line and the attackers withdrew under cover of darkness.

There were no major attacks during the 19th, by which time the defenders east of St Vith had been reinforced by the remaining two companies of the 23rd Armored Infantry Battalion while several more field artillery batteries, including two 155mm batteries from VIII Corps reserve, were now deployed inside the perimeter. By the evening of the 19th, however, the German LXVI Korps, having completed encircling two

regiments of the 106th Infantry Division in the Schnee Eifel (the 422nd and 423rd) and taking their surrender, was beginning to form up for a more serious assault on St Vith.

To the right of the 294th Volksgrenadier Regiment now appeared the 295th, with the division's Füsilier Bataillon to its right at Wallerode. The 293rd Regiment was in reserve at Schönberg, while on the left of the German line were the 190th and 164th Regiments respectively of the 62nd Volksgrenadier Division. However, the German Korps' commander, General Walter Lucht, was waiting for the arrival of the formidable Führer Begleit Brigade.

This thoroughly confused Allied intelligence because both it and the Führer Grenadier Brigade, were parts of the 'Grossdeutschland' Panzer Korps which was known to be on the Russian front! However, as things turned out, Fuller's task force on the Prümerberg heights was not immediately going to be put to the test, because Lucht planned his main assault on St Vith from the northeast. This resulted in the major battle for CCB around Hünningen and Rodt over 20-23 December.

16/12/1944	18/12	20/12	22/12	24/12	26/12	28/12	30/12	6/1/1945	13/1	20/1	27/1	3/2	7/2
pages 46-61,75-78		81-85		86-87		90-91		88-89					

U.S. XVIII CORPS' BATTLES

CCA, 7th Armored Division

Poteau – December 18-24

By midday on 18 December Brigadier-General Robert Hasbrouck had almost completely ruled out a counter-attack east of St Vith towards Schönberg. What concerned him much more was his northern flank, where 1 SS-Panzer Division was known to be operating. Colonel Warren had reported the situation at Poteau, which was now in enemy hands, so there now was also just the tiny blocking force at Petit Thier to stop a German assault on Vielsalm, where Hasbrouck had established his headquarters, leaving Bruce Clarke in charge at St Vith. CCR's 17th Tank Battalion was on its way to reinforce the front line in front of St Vith, so there was, in fact, a gaping hole in the northern perimeter with a strong force of Germans known to be around Recht.

What Hasbrouck could not suspect was that Kampfgruppe 'Hansen' had attacked at Poteau only to secure its own flank before driving on westward, but the precautions Hasbrouck was about to implement would prove decisive over the next few days because 9 SS-Panzer Division from II Korps would shortly arrive at Recht, in the wake of the Leibstandarte battlegroup.

At this point in time Colonel Dwight Rosenbaum's CCA was not really gainfully employed guarding 7th Armored Division's southern flank around Beho, and had so far seen no sign of the enemy. Accordingly, Hasbrouck ordered Rosenbaum to take the bulk of his command directly to Poteau, recapture it, and extend his line towards Rodt to the east in order to re-establish communication with CCR at St Vith. Leaving just his light tank company together with a handful of

engineers, anti-aircraft gunners and reconnaissance troops behind to watch Beho, Rosenbaum set off with the remainder of the 40th Tank Battalion and his 48th Armored Infantry Battalion just after noon.

Passing through St Vith to approach Poteau from the southeast, Rosenbaum found he faced no easy task. Hansen had left a rearguard of Panzergrenadiers and Jagdpanzers at the little road and rail junction, who were getting well dug-in as Rosenbaum's leading tank platoon approached the railway cutting from due south. The tank destroyers were hidden amongst the houses to guard the approaches from both Vielsalm and St Vith, with machine-gun positions able to give enfilading fire from the woods to either side. A platoon of Shermans and a company of infantry took all afternoon to winkle out the German positions south of the railway line, but by nightfall Rosenbaum had an entire

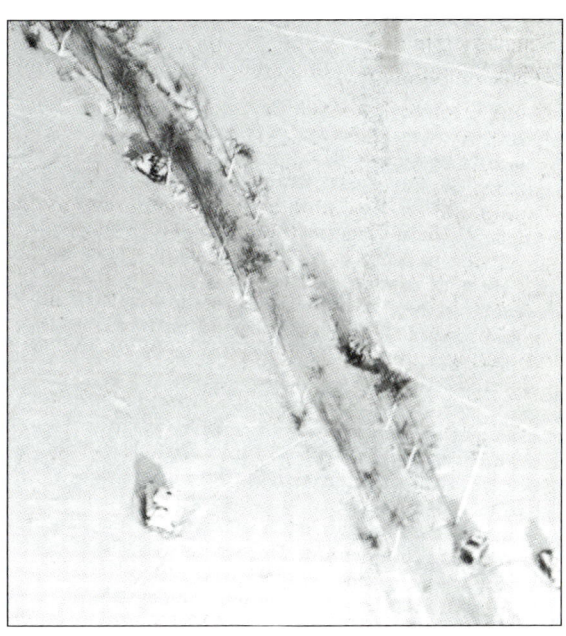

Restricted to the narrow front because of the hills and woods on either side of the road, the Panthers of 9 SS-Panzer Division fell easy prey on this occasion.
(U.S. Signal Corps)

16/12/1944	18/12	20/12	22/12	24/12	26/12	28/12	30/12	6/1/1945	13/1	20/1	27/1	3/2	7/2
pages 46-61,75-80		83-85	86-87	90-91		88-89							

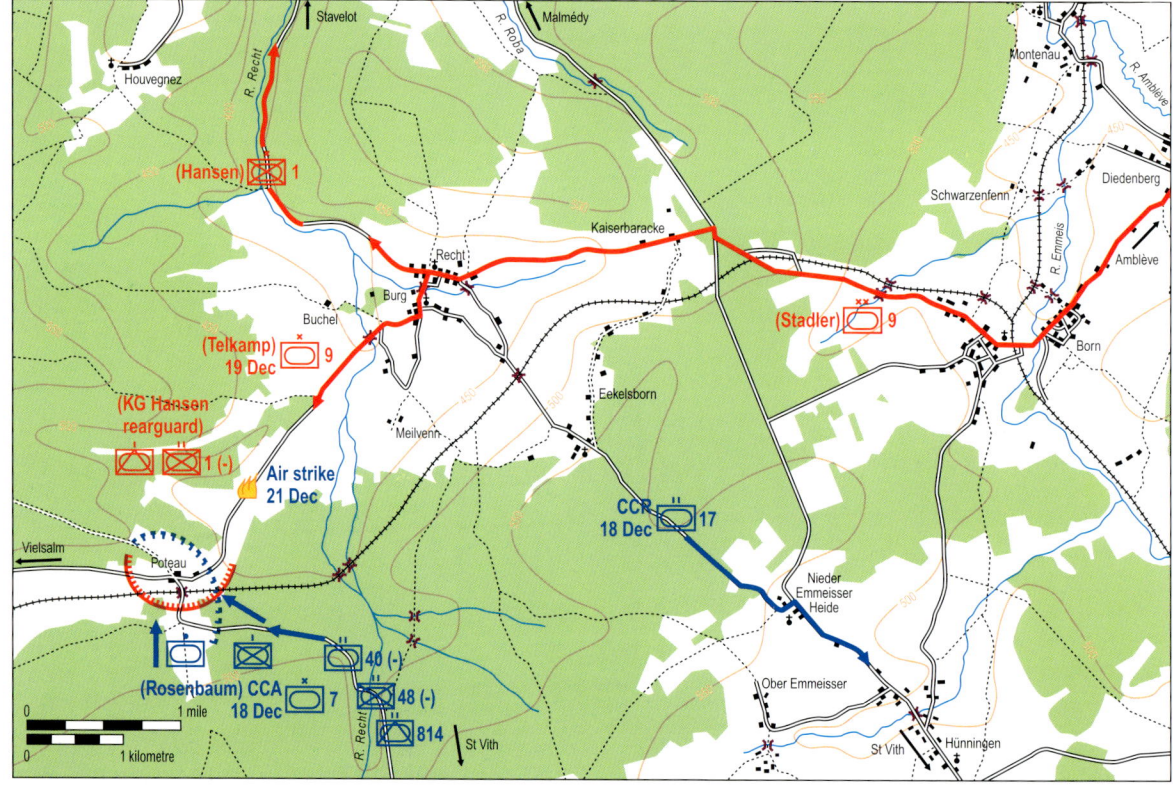

After CCA's counter-attack at Poteau against the
1 SS-Panzer Division rearguard during the afternoon
of 18 December, Rosenbaum established a defensive
perimeter (dotted) and successfully held off a
9 SS-Panzer Division battlegroup until the 21st.

company of tanks and one of infantry on the north bank
of the cutting. However, Panzergrenadiers still tena-
ciously held on to the couple of remaining houses in
the village. These were cleared early on 19 December
when a fresh threat emerged: Kampfgruppe 'Telkamp'
of 9 SS-Panzer Division.

To begin with Telkamp made no effort to take the
junction, contenting himself with infiltrating the woods
to the north with grenadiers tasked with keeping the
defenders' heads down. However, Rosenbaum had
other problems than Poteau, because on 20 December
he had to fight a major engagement with part of the
Führer Begleit Brigade towards Rodt. Poteau was still
crucial, though, as it was becoming increasingly
apparent that the St Vith salient would have to be
evacuated, and the road west to Vielsalm would have
to be protected. Rosenbaum therefore constructed a

circular defence around the hamlet and waited for the
assault to come.

Telkamp struck on the 21st, personally leading his
Panthers through the deep snow, but now the narrow
approach to Poteau came to the defenders' aid
because the Germans could not deploy more than half
a dozen tanks abreast. Rosenbaum had also reinforced the Shermans in the hamlet with some M36s
from the 814th Tank Destroyer Battalion, and a 90mm
round blew Telkamp's tank from under him. He tried to
rally his men, but as four more tanks were picked off
one by one, he called off the assault.

Over the next two days he contented himself with
keeping the defenders pinned, but on Christmas Eve,
in concert with a determined German push all
around the rapidly-decreasing American perimeter, he
attacked once more. Now, Rosenbaum received
unexpected aid from a flight of P38s which strafed and
bombed Telkamp's Panthers. This timely intervention
halted the attack and left Rosenbaum free to evacuate
his command back through Vielsalm, his task finished;
CCA was the last major American unit in the north to
break free.

16/12/1944	18/12	20/12	22/12	24/12	26/12	28/12	30/12	6/1/1945	13/1	20/1	27/1	3/2	7/2
pages 46-61,75-80		83-85	86-87	90-91		88-89							

U.S. XVIII CORPS' BATTLES

CCB, 7th Armored Division

Hünningen and Rodt – December 18-24

German troops – the 18th Füsilier Bataillon of the 18th Volksgrenadier Division with about ten StuG assault guns and a company of pioniers – approached St Vith from the northeast on the evening of 17 December and established themselves in the village of Wallerode, overlooking the valley road from Schönberg to St Vith from the north. At about the same time Brigadier-General Bruce Clarke was deploying the leading elements of 7th Armored Division's CCB into a defensive line stretching from Prümerberg to Hünningen.

At about 0800 hrs on 18 December the Füsiliers launched a reconnaissance in force towards Hünningen. At the time this approach route was covered only by A and C Troops of the 87th Cavalry Reconnaissance Squadron and a handful of M15 half-tracks with quad .50 machine-guns. A call for help brought two companies of Shermans and a company of tank destroyers from CCB of 9th Armored Division which chased the Germans back before they were relieved by a freshly-arrived company of M4s from Lieutenant-Colonel Robert Erlenbusch's 31st Tank Battalion, 7th Armored Division's CCB.

Describing the defence of St Vith, the U.S. official history notes that, 'The homogeneity of the battalion, in American practice the basic tactical unit, largely ceased to exist, nor did time and the enemy ever permit any substantial regrouping to restore this unity'. The whole battle was like that, with units thrown in piecemeal to counter-act local threats, often not knowing whom they were supposed to be taking orders from, where they were supposed to be going or what they were supposed to be doing except fight Germans. Fortunately, for the most part, their officers were quite happy to acquiesce with local needs and rank almost ceased to matter, with seniors quite content to accept tactical orders from juniors. This was especially true within veteran divisions such as the 7th Armored. Brigadier-General Robert Hasbrouck wrote afterwards that 'I never knew who was in my command; I just did everything I thought necessary'. A typical example of such flexibility is when Lieutenant-Colonel Fred Warren, in temporary command of CCR at Poteau, did not demur when Lieutenant-Colonel John Wemple's 17th Tank Battalion was snatched away from him to reinforce CCB east of St Vith. Thus, by the night of 19 December, an improvised but effective defensive perimeter was rapidly taking shape.

St Vith had originally been relatively unimportant to the Germans: I SS-Panzer Corps' Rollbahns ran to the north and those of XLVII Panzer Korps to the south. But with the failure of the former to achieve a decisive breakthrough it became a nexus, and on 18 December Model released the Führer Begleit Brigade – a reinforced armoured brigade – from reserve to help the Volksgrenadiers get rid of this ulcer on both his flanks. Given the distance to travel from Daun via Prüm it could not possibly arrive in much less than 48 hours, by which time its commander, Oberst Otto Remer, had reconnoitred the St Vith perimeter. Remer decided that the best chance of success lay in attacking from the northeast in the Wallerode-Hünningen sector protected by CCB of 7th Armored Division.

On the afternoon of 20 December, covered by fog, Remer launched his first assault against Hünningen before his full brigade had arrived, but his leading four tanks were knocked out by M36s of the 814th Tank Destroyer Battalion and he abandoned the effort. Earlier in the day, an assault by the Füsiliers in Wallerode had been met by furious artillery fire and the commander of the 18th Volksgrenadier Division, Oberst Günther von Hoffmann-Schönborn who personally led the attack, was wounded. But this was just the beginning for 7th Armored's CCB.

16/12/1944	18/12	20/12	22/12	24/12	26/12	28/12	30/12	6/1/1945	13/1	20/1	27/1	3/2	7/2
pages 46-61,75-80		81-82	86-87	90-91		88-89							

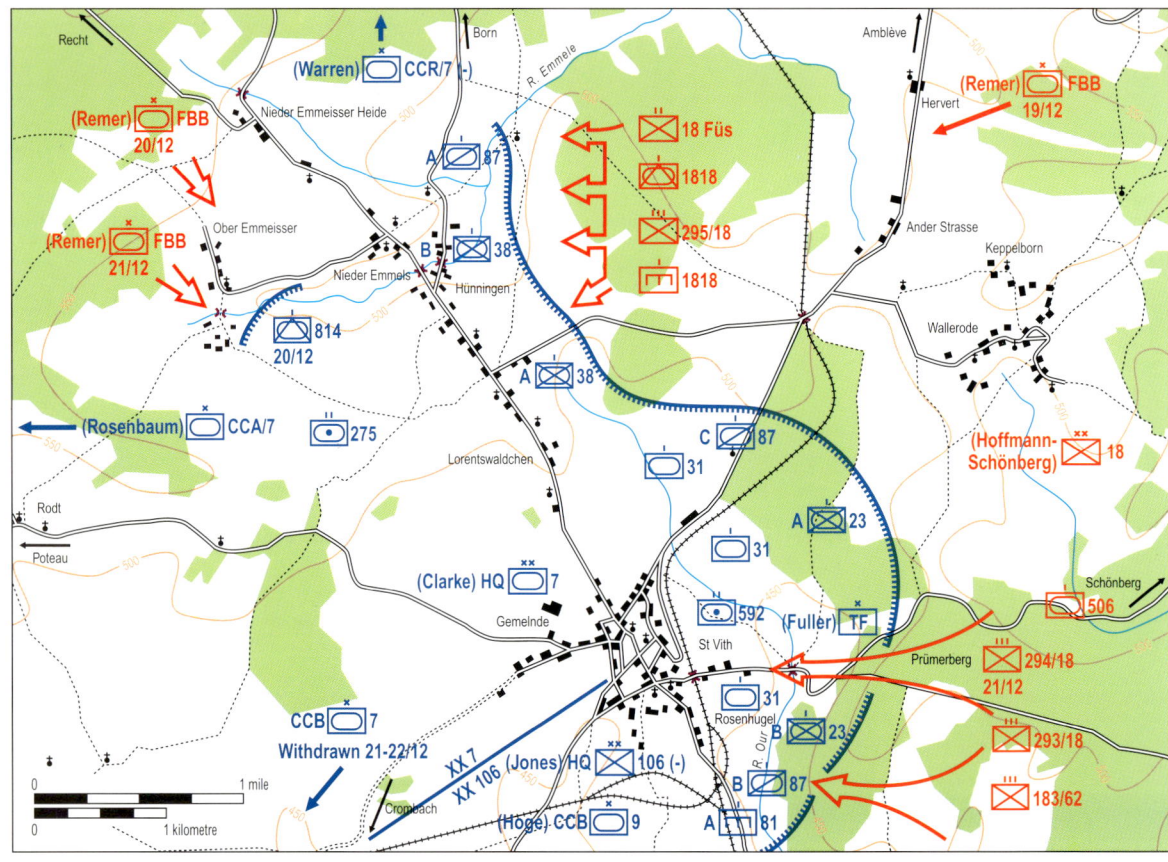

After successfully repelling attacks over 19–20 December, CCB was finally outflanked on the 21st when 18 Volksgrenadier Division broke through into St Vith.

Next day Otto Remer, still lacking most of his tanks, tried a probing attack west of Büllingen at Rodt (on Belgian maps, Sart-lez-St Vith), but this was repulsed by Dwight Rosenbaum's CCA. Meanwhile, the 18th Volksgrenadier Division was launching a major assault towards Hünningen which, at this time, was defended only by the wing of Lieutenant-Colonel William Fuller's task force running north from Prümerberg. This wing consisted of two companies of infantry from the 38th Battalion, one from the 23rd and a troop from the 87th Cavalry Squadron. The German artillery barrage was the worst the battle-hardened men of 7th Armored Division had ever experienced, and was only partially alleviated by counter-battery fire called down urgently from the guns deployed west of St Vith. Then the Volksgrenadiers attacked in groups of about 40 or 50 men, using the woods for cover. They were unable to break through but, further south, their 294th Regiment finally succeeded in their assault along the Schönberg road through the Prümerberg heights. During this engagement the valiant first commander of the defenders, Tom Riggs, was killed.

The Volksgrenadiers now poured into St Vith itself, outflanking Fuller's men around Hünningen. Fuller himself, who had not slept since arriving on 17 December, had to be relieved by Lieutenant-Colonel Robert Rhea, CO of 23rd Armored Infantry Battalion.

Still retaining a foothold in Hünningen, Rhea pulled the right of his line back to conform with the general move back west of St Vith. However, the American situation was deteriorating rapidly, especially with the unexpected news that 2 SS-Panzer Division – which was not thought to be anywhere in the vicinity – was probing for weak spots on the southern flank of the perimeter.

Major-General Matthew Ridgway who, as commander of XVIII (Airborne) Corps, had assumed overall responsibility for the defence of St Vith and had been

16/12/1944	18/12	20/12	22/12	24/12	26/12	28/12	30/12	6/1/1945	13/1	20/1	27/1	3/2	7/2
pages 46-61,75-80		81-82	86-87	90-91		88-89							

Shermans of CCB, supporting the 23rd Armored Infantry Battalion, on the alert outside St Vith. Close collaboration between armour and infantry was a key factor in the rapid American come-back after the reverses of the first ten days of the Ardennes campaign. (U.S. National Archives)

ordered by Montgomery to evacuate the salient, began moving the most southern forces out through Salmchâteau. First went CCB of 9th Armored Division, followed by the two surviving regiments of the 28th and 106th Infantry Divisions, the 112th and 424th, leaving just a task force under Lieutenant-Colonel Robert Jones to cover their retreat (which was to have unforeseen results when he was ambushed as he tried to withdraw his own men).

In the north, meanwhile, CCB of 7th Armored was having a desperate struggle to maintain any semblance of a line as it slowly retreated towards Vielsalm. Remer's Führer Begleit Brigade had captured Rodt after an earlier skirmish with CCA, which had then withdrawn to Poteau. Clarke brought CCB back now to new positions around the hamlets of Hinderhausen and Crombach. By this time, though, it was not an organised Combat Command but small groups of individual soldiers and tanks fighting for survival. Hasbrouck sent a memo to Ridgway saying that the withdrawal had been 'expensive'. 'So far', he wrote, 'we are missing at least one half of Clarke's force', but added, 'of course, many of them will show

up but they will be minus weapons, ammunition, blankets and rations as well as at a low physical level.' Fortunately, the German pursuit from St Vith was as clogged with traffic jams as 7th Armored Division's own advance there had been on 17 December.

At this point, in the early hours of 23 December, the Führer Begleit Brigade struck CCB's northern sector at Crombach, attacking down the railway line and outflanking the defenders at Poteau. Using flares to illuminate the tanks of John Wemple's 17th Battalion, they were undeterred by shellfire from the 434th Armored Field Artillery Battalion near Hinderhausen and were soon in the village with Panzerfausts. By dawn, both sides could lay claim to Crombach, but Wemple had no desire to stay and at dawn on the 23rd, with movement helped by a sharp frost, he broke out to the west, the infantry riding on the decks of the tanks firing wildly at anything that moved. The U.S. official history records laconically that 'the rest of the journey...was without incident'.

CCB's defence at Hünningen was typical of many engagements during the first week of the battle when sheer determination proved superior to firepower.

U.S. XVIII CORPS' BATTLES
2nd Battalion, 325th Glider Infantry Regiment

Baraque Fraiture – December 23

After the evacuation of the St Vith salient into the welcoming arms of the 82nd Airborne Division, XVIII Corps' commander Matthew Ridgway faced a new problem which had initially been raised by skirmishes with 2 SS-Panzer Division south of the perimeter. These had culminated in one of its Kampfgruppen cutting off and virtually annihilating a rearguard task force at Salmchâteau. The remainder of the SS division, further to the south, was still heading west, although apparently delayed by fuel shortages which gave Ridgway a little time to adjust his lines.

A critical geographical feature on the SS division's westward march was the crossroads at Baraque Fraiture, which lies on one of the highest hills in the Ardennes. Even before the evacuation of St Vith became necessary, the CO of 7th Armored Division, Robert Hasbrouck, realised its potential importance, and as early as 19 December had begun building a scratch defensive force. First to arrive were three 105mm howitzers commanded by Major Arthur C. Parker of the 589th Field Artillery Battalion which had got separated from their parent 106th Infantry Division. Next day Hasbrouck added four half-tracks from 7th Armored's 203rd Anti-Aircraft Auto-Weapons Battalion.

The first attack at what became known as 'Parker's Crossroads' came before dawn on 21 December, when a company from the 560th Volksgrenadier Division stumbled accidentally on the position and was cut to pieces by the quad .50 machine-guns on the M15s. Amongst the dead and prisoners was an officer

from 2 SS-Panzer Division, which prompted Hasbrouck to send D Troop of his 87th Cavalry Reconnaissance Squadron to reinforce the crossroads.

The Volksgrenadiers kept the defenders alert for the rest of the day with intermittent mortar fire which wounded Parker so Major Elliott Goldstein, also of the 589th, took over. Nothing more happened here on the 22nd apart from the arrival of 11 M4 Shermans and two M7 'Priests' detached from 3rd Armored Division's Task Force 'Kane', but with the fall of St Vith, Baraque Fraiture suddenly began to assume greater importance. Nevertheless, under pressure elsewhere, Kane had to withdraw his tanks in the afternoon, leaving just the 'Priests' behind.

The 82nd Airborne Division CO, James Gavin, now ordered Colonel Charles Billingslea, commander of the 325th Glider Infantry Regiment, to send Major Richard Gibson's 2nd Battalion to Fraiture. Billingslea deployed D and E Companies on high ground behind the village itself a mile away and sent Captain Junior R. Woodruff's F Company to the crossroads. The SS

Unwitting lambs to the slaughter, men of Captain Junior Woodruff's 'F' Company, II/325th Glider Infantry Regiment, advance towards Baraque Fraiture.
(U.S. Signal Corps)

16/12/1944	18/12	20/12	22/12	24/12	26/12	28/12	30/12	6/1/1945	13/1	20/1	27/1	3/2	7/2
pages 46-61,75-80		81-85		90-91		88-89							

The situation at Fraiture and Baraque Fraiture during the morning of 23 December prior to the arrival of the second SS battalion and of the troop of Shermans from Manhay which had to fight through small groups of Panzergrenadiers in the woods. The German victory here threatened the junction between XVIII and VII Corps but 2 SS-Panzer Division was unable to break through at Grandmenil.

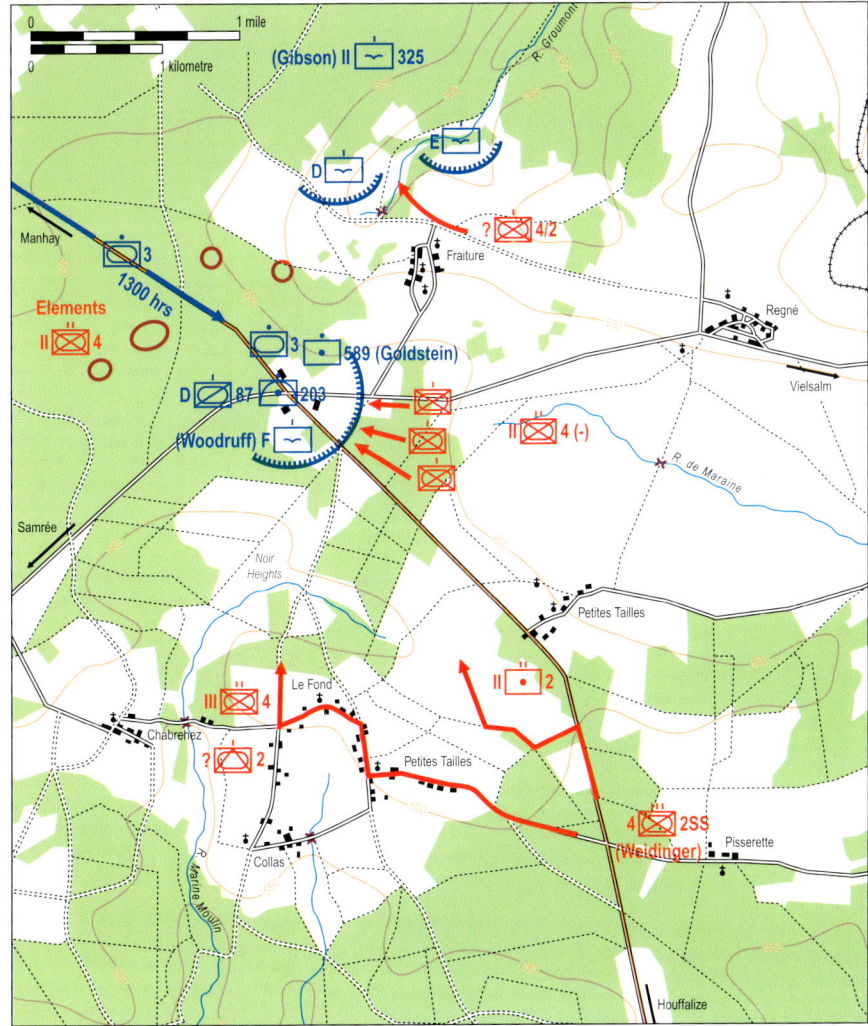

assault began before daylight on 23 December with a company-size attack against the paras at Fraiture, which was beaten off; the German commander then contented himself with leaving a blocking force in the village, pending the arrival of the Führer Begleit Brigade next day, to prevent Gibson from interfering in the main action. The remaining three companies of the German battalion, meanwhile, launched an assault from the southeast towards the crossroads, which again was repulsed.

Later that morning, while the Germans kept the crossroads under mortar and artillery fire, Goldstein drove to Manhay to appeal for help from CCA of 3rd Armored Division, but all that could be spared was a platoon of five Shermans which reached the crossroads at 1300 hrs. The main German assault started three hours later with one battalion of Panzer-grenadiers supported by a company of PzKpfw IVs approaching from the southeast, while a second battalion with a company of assault guns attacked from the west. Four German tanks were knocked out by the Shermans and a fifth by a well-placed round from one of the 105mm howitzers, but as the Panzergrenadiers swarmed all over the glider infantry foxholes, the remaining three M4s retreated.

With bitter hand-to-hand fighting all around him, Woodruff appealed for permission to withdraw, but Billingslea to begin with refused. When he relented after darkness had fallen, Woodruff's men broke through the German cordon into the woods to the northwest. From an initial strength of 116 men, there were just 44 survivors.

16/12/1944	18/12	20/12	22/12	24/12	26/12	28/12	30/12	6/1/1945	13/1	20/1	27/1	3/2	7/2
pages 46-61,75-80		81-85		90-91		88-89							

U.S. XVIII CORPS' BATTLES

509th Parachute Infantry Regiment

Sadzot-Erezée – December 28-29

By 21 December 1944, when it was ordered from a rest area at Epernay, France, to report for duty with XVIII (Airborne) Corps in Belgium, the 509th Parachute Infantry Battalion was the most experienced in the U.S. Army. Indeed, many of the men must have felt they had already done 'their bit' and resented being dragged from soft beds to a foxhole in the snow. They would, in fact, suffer such high casualties in the Ardennes that the battalion would have to be disbanded on 1 March 1945.

Like the 1st Infantry Division which had previously encountered the Germans at Kasserine, the 509th had also seen action in North Africa. Originally numbered 503rd, the battalion was renumbered after it arrived in England in June 1942 and, commanded by Lieutenant-Colonel Edson Raff (now CO of the 507th Parachute Infantry Regiment), had jumped south of Oran on 7 November 1942 in order to seize two airfields in advance of the ground forces. In July 1943, attached to the 82nd Airborne Division, the battalion also jumped during the invasion of Sicily, then at Avellino in support of the Salerno landings, then in August 1944 on the Mediterranean coast of France during operation 'Anvil'.

Now, in December 1944, commanded by Major Edmund Tomasik, the 509th found itself on the right of the 82nd Airborne Division's flank, loosely attached to the 508th Parachute Infantry Regiment which had helped cover the withdrawal from the St Vith salient. The 508th had already had one fierce encounter with the 19th SS-Panzergrenadier Regiment west of Vielsalm on Christmas Day while covering the 82nd Airborne's withdrawal to the new, shorter, line established by Ridgway as a prelude to VII Corps' planned counter-attack.

On 27 December, Tomasik's 509th was positioned near Erezée slightly behind Colonel Douglas Smith's 289th Regiment of the 75th Infantry Division, itself newly-arrived in the Ardennes. Unfortunately, in deploying the regiment through the woods southwest of Grandmenil in support of 3rd Armored Division, Smith had inadvertently allowed a thousand-yard gap to develop between I and III/289th around the tiny hamlet of Sadzot. And it was just here, equally inadvertently, that a kampfgruppe of 2 SS-Panzer Division commanded by SS-Sturmbannführer Ernst-August Krag launched its assault in the early hours of 28 December. (It was this kampfgruppe which had virtually destroyed Task Force 'Jones' at Salmchâteau five days earlier.)

The kampfgruppe comprised a reconnaissance and a tank destroyer battalion reinforced by the three battalions of 25 SS-Panzergrenadier Regiment, and its sudden appearance in Sadzot at about 0200 hrs, having made its way through the forest undetected by the American battalions either side, came as a

Paratroops from the 82nd Airborne Division follow an M10 tank destroyer past a German tank which has shed a track.
(U.S. Signal Corps)

16/12/1944	18/12	20/12	22/12	24/12	26/12	28/12	30/12	6/1/1945	13/1	20/1	27/1	3/2	7/2
pages 46-61,75-80		81-85	86-87	90-91									

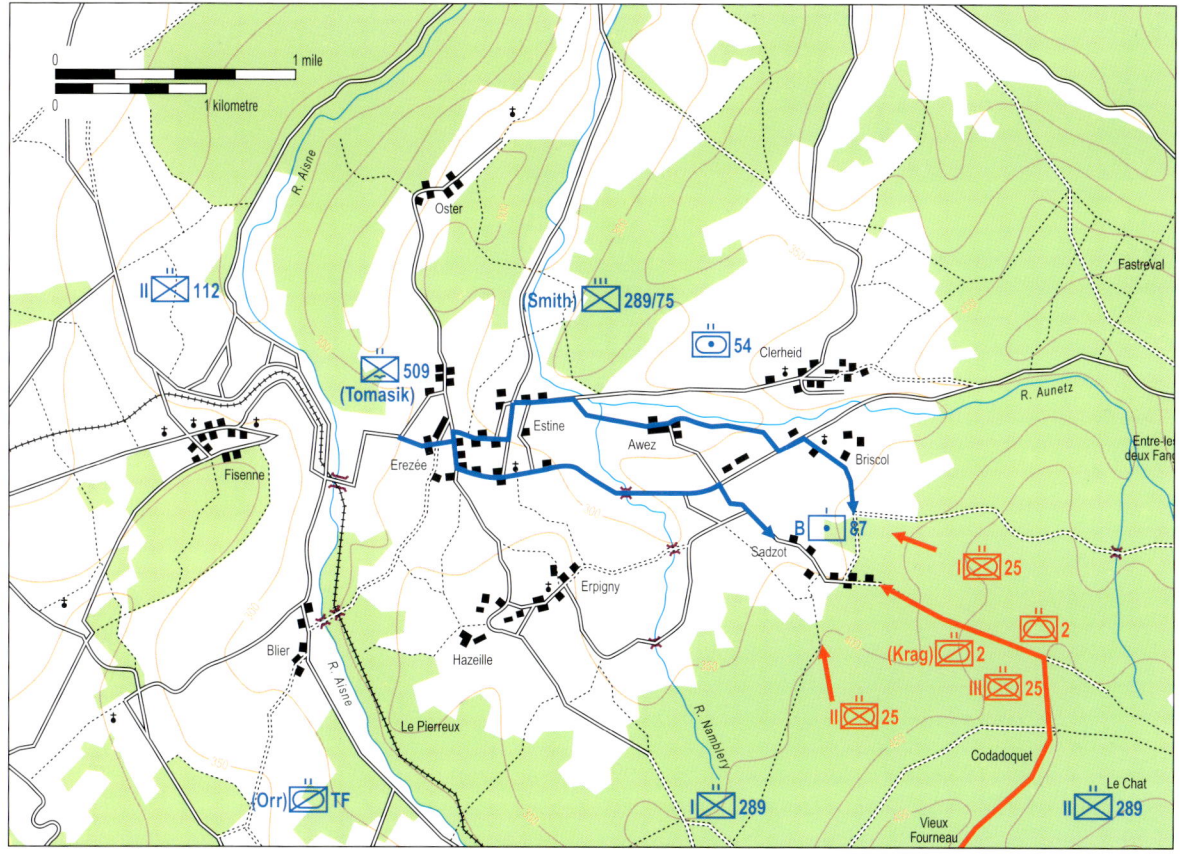

Sadzot was manned by only a single mortar company at the time of the German attack. Tomasik's two-pronged counter-attack against far superior forces succeeded through sheer surprise.

complete surprise. Artillery fire from the 54th Armored Field Artillery Battalion north of the village was quickly brought into play and Tomasik's 509th Battalion was roused to counter-attack.

The ensuing battle in pitch darkness through the densely-packed trees around the village and across the stream which bisects it was, as the U.S. official history records, 'a soldiers' battle'. It was a night of total confusion as squads and platoons fired at shadows, so intermingled that at one point the German commander actually put down mortar fire on his own men. In Sadzot itself, the 509th quickly captured the northern side of the village and called down artillery fire on the remaining defenders, encircling them and forcing their surrender as day broke. By 1100 hrs Sadzot was back in American hands but the battle was not yet over.

Later in the day, the 2nd Battalion of the 112th Regiment, ex-28th Infantry Division, was sent in to plug the gap between the two battalions of the 289th, but got lost. Believing it was in position, Brigadier-General Doyle Hickey launched the 509th in a counter-attack early on 29 December supported by six M5 light tanks, but Krag chose the same moment to launch another assault on Sadzot. His anti-tank guns took out three of the American tanks and the remainder, accompanied by Tomasik's paras, fell back – but so did the surprised Germans.

Eventually II/112th did get into its proper position and at dusk Hickey ordered it into another attack, spearheaded by Tomasik's paras. This finally forced Krag to abandon any idea of renewing an assault through Erezée and by dawn on 30 December the American line was secure. However, the 509th had lost no fewer than 120 men out of the 745 they had started with, and by the time St Vith was recaptured on 23 January that number had reached 680.

16/12/1944	18/12	20/12	22/12	24/12	26/12	28/12	30/12	6/1/1945	13/1	20/1	27/1	3/2	7/2
pages 46-61,75-80		81-85	86-87	90-91									

U.S. XVIII CORPS' BATTLES

505th Parachute Infantry Regiment

The Salm Sector – December 21-25

Freshly-arrived at Werbomont on 19 December, Colonel William Ekman's 505th Parachute Infantry Regiment was promptly despatched to cover the bridges over the Salm and Amblève at Trois Ponts. No-one at this time knew that the small force of engineers there had successfully denied passage to Kampfgruppe 'Peiper' the previous day by blowing the bridges, a discovery which came as a pleasant surprise in a week full of nasty ones. On the 505th's left, Colonel Reuben Tucker positioned his 504th at Rahier, while Colonel Roy Lindquist's 508th was stationed to the rear as a reserve. Next day, patrols from the 504th established contact with the 119th Infantry Regiment near Stoumont while, to the south, the 505th similarly met up with a reconnaissance troop from 7th Armored Division southwest of Trois Ponts at Fosse. Ekman now consolidated the line by putting II/505th in Trois Ponts and establishing a bridgehead there on the east bank of the Salm.

The Corps' commander, Matthew Ridgway, at this time intended that the 504th and 505th would move east, the 504th through Cheneux and the 505th towards Stavelot. With 3rd Armored Division moving in from the northwest, this would encircle, and ensure the final destruction of, Kampfgruppe 'Peiper'. However, I/504th was decimated when it attacked at Cheneux and another threat quickly emerged. The commander of 1 SS-Panzer Division, under orders to go to the relief of Kampfgruppe 'Peiper', had brought his most southerly battlegroup, that commanded by SS-Standartenführer Max Hansen, north from its intended Rollbahn after its encounter with 7th Armored Division at Recht-Poteau, and by 21 December it had reached Wanne. Hansen now began probing along the four-mile front established by the 505th between Trois Ponts and Grand Halleux.

His first attack hit Lieutenant-Colonel Benjamin Vandervoort's II/505th at Trois Ponts. E Company, on the far side of the river, was over-run by Panzer-grenadiers supported by assault guns, even though bazookas took a toll, and Vandervoort sent F Company across in support. Their single 57mm antitank gun was soon knocked out, just as the one defending the railway underpass had been on 18 December. Vandervoort had been unable to raise his regimental commander on radio but, fortuitously, Ekman now arrived on the scene and promptly ordered the withdrawal of the survivors on the far side of the river. Many jumped into the water pursued by German grenadiers who gained a very brief foothold on the west bank of the Salm before they were thrown back. III/505th to the south, meanwhile, was fighting off another attack at La Neuville where the bridge over the Salm remained intact. However, as a column of tanks and infantry approached from the east, the battalion blew the bridge and called down artillery fire, and the enemy withdrew into the gathering night.

The following day, 22 December, Kampfgruppe 'Hansen' made only limited probing attacks at the 505th's lines. The odd platoons which got across the river were promptly tossed back into the water, and an assault by two companies of Panzergrenadiers across the still-intact bridge at Grand Halleux disintegrated when the paras blew the bridge while the Germans were in the middle of it. There were no further attacks on the 505th sector during 23 December, because Kampfgruppe 'Hansen' was trying to find another way to the relief of Kampfgruppe 'Peiper' at La Gleize, but this day the German battlegroup met its end at the hands of 3rd Armored and 30th Infantry Divisions and only about a thousand men managed to escape back to the southeast.

On Christmas Eve the situation remained much the same, with the 504th on the north of the 82nd Airborne's line, the 505th in the centre and the 508th

16/12/1944	18/12	20/12	22/12	24/12	26/12	28/12	30/12	6/1/1945	13/1	20/1	27/1	3/2	7/2
pages 46-61,75-80		81-85	86-87			88-89							

Four miles is a long stretch to defend with a single regiment but the 505th beat back Hansen's grenadiers at Trois Ponts, La Neuville and Grand Halleux. As a final footnote, the survivors of Kampfgruppe 'Peiper' brushed against the paras' northern flank during the night of 24-25 December. After a brief firefight the two groups continued passing in the night in opposite directions, although Ekman later regretted having missed an opportunity of capturing Peiper.

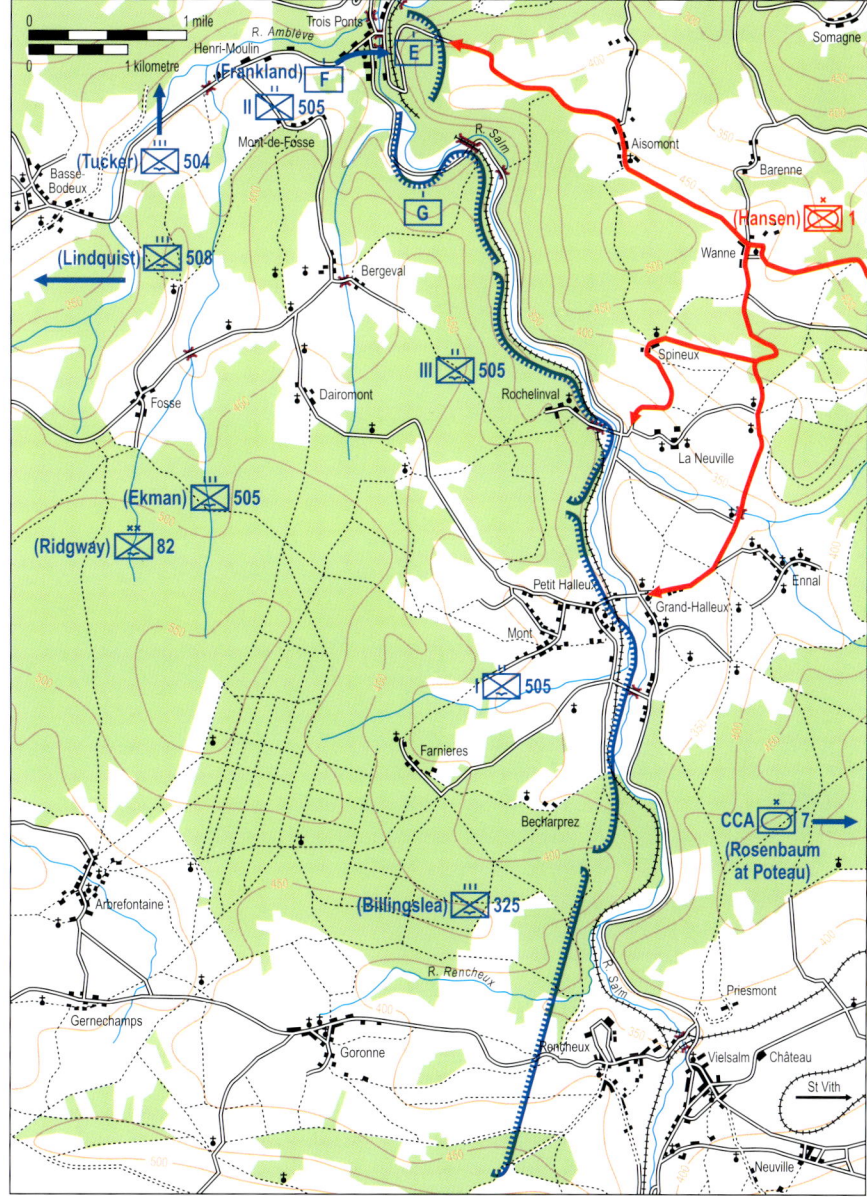

now extended on their right. On the far right Colonel Charles Billingslea's 325th Glider Infantry Regiment had linked up with elements of 7th Armored Division around Vielsalm and continued the line to where the 2nd Battalion defended Fraiture and the crossroads at Baraque Fraiture. Further west, the 75th Infantry Division was moving into the line, to reinforce CCR of 3rd Armored Division. However, the 82nd's commander, Major-General James Gavin, was not happy with the situation and met Ekman and his other regimental commanders at Ekman's command post in Trois Ponts. He knew he faced elements of at least three Panzer divisions (1, 2 and 9 SS) and his defence was stretched far too thinly. He therefore decided to keep Trois Ponts as the northern anchor point and withdraw to a new, shorter, line stretching from there to Manhay, dig in and sow minefields. The planned withdrawal was accomplished with professional skill within 24 hours.

16/12/1944	18/12	20/12	22/12	24/12	26/12	28/12	30/12	6/1/1945	13/1	20/1	27/1	3/2	7/2
pages 46-61,75-80		81-85	86-87			88-89							

THE ALLIED AIR FORCE

Forty-Eight Hours!

Forty-eight hours! Not a long time, but on this occasion, long enough. That is the delay, overall, which it is estimated the combined U.S. Eighth and Ninth Air Forces, and Royal Air Force Bomber and Fighter Commands, caused to the German Ardennes offensive. But those 48 hours, totalled over the 18 days between the beginning of the German offensive on 16 December 1944, and the beginning of the real Allied riposte on 3 January 1945, were decisive.

It is axiomatic that successful military campaigns depend much more upon surprise and speed of execution than 'big battalions'. The Germans achieved the former most successfully, and had 'bigger battalions' deployed at the key points as well. But it was time they lost, partly due to faulty planning and logistics, partly due to the terrain and the weather, partly due to the sheer courage and stubborness of the PBI in their snow-covered foxholes, partly due to the speed of SHAEF's response once the shape of the threat was perceived, and partly due to those precious 48 hours gained overall by Allied aircrews.

After their bitter experience in Normandy, where the rocket-firing Allied fighter-bombers enjoyed a turkey shoot against the Panzers, the Germans deliberately planned their offensive for a time of year when low cloud, falling snow and thick fog would mask much of their movements from aerial observation and attack. Having said that, it is difficult to see how they could have launched the operation at any other time: it would have been impossible earlier, even though Hitler did originally intend it to take place in November; and any later would have been too late.

The way things actually turned out, Allied air attacks on the Panzer spearheads in the First Army sector during the first week of the offensive were relatively ineffectual in terms of inflicting matériel damage, as the two-hour operation against Kampfgruppe 'Peiper' on the afternoon of 18 December typifies. As soon as reports that the battlegroup was passing through Stavelot reached First Army headquarters in Spa,

Brigadier-General Elwood R. 'Pete' Quesada commanded IX Tactical Air Command in support of First Army from D-Day. (U.S. Signal Corps)

Hodges telephoned Brigadier-General Elwood 'Pete' Quesada at IX Tactical Air Force HQ in Verviers and asked him to try to locate the direction in which the column was heading.

Because there was low cloud over the region, the CO of Quesada's 67th Tactical Reconnaissance Group, Colonel George Peck, asked for volunteers. Two pilots stepped forward and were promptly in the air heading for the Amblève valley. Conditions were hazardous: in order to get under the cloud, the pilots had to fly at less than 100 feet – below the level of the surrounding hills – but they did locate Peiper's column which by this time, having been turned back at Trois Ponts, was heading towards Werbomont via La Gleize and Cheneux.

Quesada now ordered up the 365th and 368th Fighter Groups, 70th Fighter Wing, which soon had 32 P-47 Thunderbolts in the air, carrying 500lb bombs. The aircraft attacked in two waves, flying in flights of four, and bombed and strafed the whole battlegroup from Cheneux back to Stavelot, where they caught the tail of the column just as the 1st Battalion of the 117th Infantry Regiment was approaching the town for a grandstand view. Having been alerted by the earlier reconnaissance flight, Peiper's flak gunners were thoroughly awake and the quad 20mm Flakvierlings crippled one aircraft, which crashed near Francorchamps, as well as damaging three others.

After the sortie, the Thunderbolt pilots reported 32 German tanks and 56 other vehicles destroyed –

U.S. NINTH AIR FORCE
(Lieutenant-General Hoyt S. Vandenberg)

IX TACTICAL AIR COMMAND
(Brigadier-General Elwood R. Quesada)

70th Fighter Wing
  365th Fighter Group (16 x P-47 Thunderbolt)
  366th Fighter Group (16 x P-47 Thunderbolt)
  367th Fighter Group (16 x P-38 Lightning)
  368th Fighter Group (16 x P-47 Thunderbolt)
  370th Fighter Group (16 x P-38 Lightning)
  474th Fighter Group (16 x P-38 Lightning)
  67th Tactical Reconnaissance Group (F-6 Mustang)
  422nd Night Fighter Squadron (Douglas P-70)

XIX TACTICAL AIR COMMAND
(Major-General Otto P. Weyland)

100th Fighter Wing
  354th Fighter Group (16 x P-47 Thunderbolt)
  358th Fighter Group (16 x P-47 Thunderbolt)
  362nd Fighter Group (16 x P-47 Thunderbolt)
  405th Fighter Group (16 x P-47 Thunderbolt)
  406th Fighter Group (16 x P-47 Thunderbolt)
  10th Photo Reconnaissance Group (Douglas F-3)
  425th Night Fighter Squadron (Douglas P-70)

XXIX TACTICAL AIR COMMAND
(Brigadier-General Richard E. Nugent)

84th Fighter Wing
  36th Fighter Group (16 x P-47 Thunderbolt)
  48th Fighter Group (16 x P-47 Thunderbolt)
  373rd Fighter Group (16 x P-47 Thunderbolt)
  404th Fighter Group (16 x P-47 Thunderbolt)

303rd Fighter Wing
  363rd Fighter Group (16 x P-51 Mustang)

IX BOMBARDMENT COMMAND
(Brigadier-General Samuel E. Anderson)

97th Combat Bomb Wing
  409th Bomb Group (A-26 Invader)
  410th Bomb Group (A-20 Havoc)
  416th Bomb Group (A-20 Havoc)

98th Combat Bomb Wing
  323rd Bomb Group (B-26 Invader)
  387th Bomb Group (B-26 Invader)
  394th Bomb Group (B-26 Invader)
  397th Bomb Group (B-26 Invader)
  1st Pathfinder Squadron (B-26 Invader)

99th Combat Bomb Wing
  322nd Bomb Group (B-26 Invader)
  344th Bomb Group (B-26 Invader)
  386th Bomb Group (B-26 Invader)
  391st Bomb Group (B-26 Invader)

IX TROOP CARRIER COMMAND
(Brigadier-General Benjamin F. Giles)

52nd Troop Carrier Command
  61st Troop Carrier Group (C-47 Skytrain)
  313th Troop Carrier Group (C-47 Skytrain)
  314th Troop Carrier Group (C-47 Skytrain)
  315th Troop Carrier Group (C-47 Skytrain)
  349th Troop Carrier Group (C-47 Skytrain)

53rd Troop Carrier Command
  434th Troop Carrier Group (C-47 Skytrain)
  435th Troop Carrier Group (C-47 Skytrain)
  436th Troop Carrier Group (C-47 Skytrain)
  437th Troop Carrier Group (C-47 Skytrain)
  438th Troop Carrier Group (C-47 Skytrain)

50th Troop Carrier Command
  439th Troop Carrier Group (C-47 Skytrain)
  440th Troop Carrier Group (C-47 Skytrain)
  441st Troop Carrier Group (C-47 Skytrain)
  442nd Troop Carrier Group (C-47 Skytrain)

though some accounts imply that the USAAF virtually won the 'battle of the bulge' single-handed! In fact, only two Panthers were destroyed, one at Stavelot, and a third damaged near the bridge at Cheneux. The latter blocked the road, and it took two hours to get a Bergepanther to remove it, delaying Peiper's advance sufficiently that Army engineers just had time to blow the next bridge at Habiémont. Those two hours proved vital in ensuring the destruction of Kampfgruppe 'Peiper' a few days later – two hours out of that total of 48 which thwarted Hitler's grandiose scheme.

Although aerial reconnaissance had an important role to play in this and other tactical encounters during the battle, and the spotter 'planes attached to each field artillery group were invaluable in pinpointing German positions for the gunners, in the area of strategic reconnaissance the Ninth Air Force rather let First Army down in the days preceding 16 December. It was this lack, as much as the absence of 'Ultra' decrypts, which helped allow the Germans to assemble the forces for their assault in such secrecy. However, in fairness to Peck's 67th Tactical Recon-naissance Group, the demands on their services elsewhere meant that there were few aircraft or pilots available to reconnoitre the 'quiet' Malmédy region before the attack began.

Because the Germans had successfully convinced Allied intelligence that their main blow was going to fall in the Aachen sector northwest of Köln, the 67th was required to keep a close watch on this region. Thus, although the Group flew 361 sorties during the month before the German attack, the Eifel region was assigned a low priority, and between 10-15 December

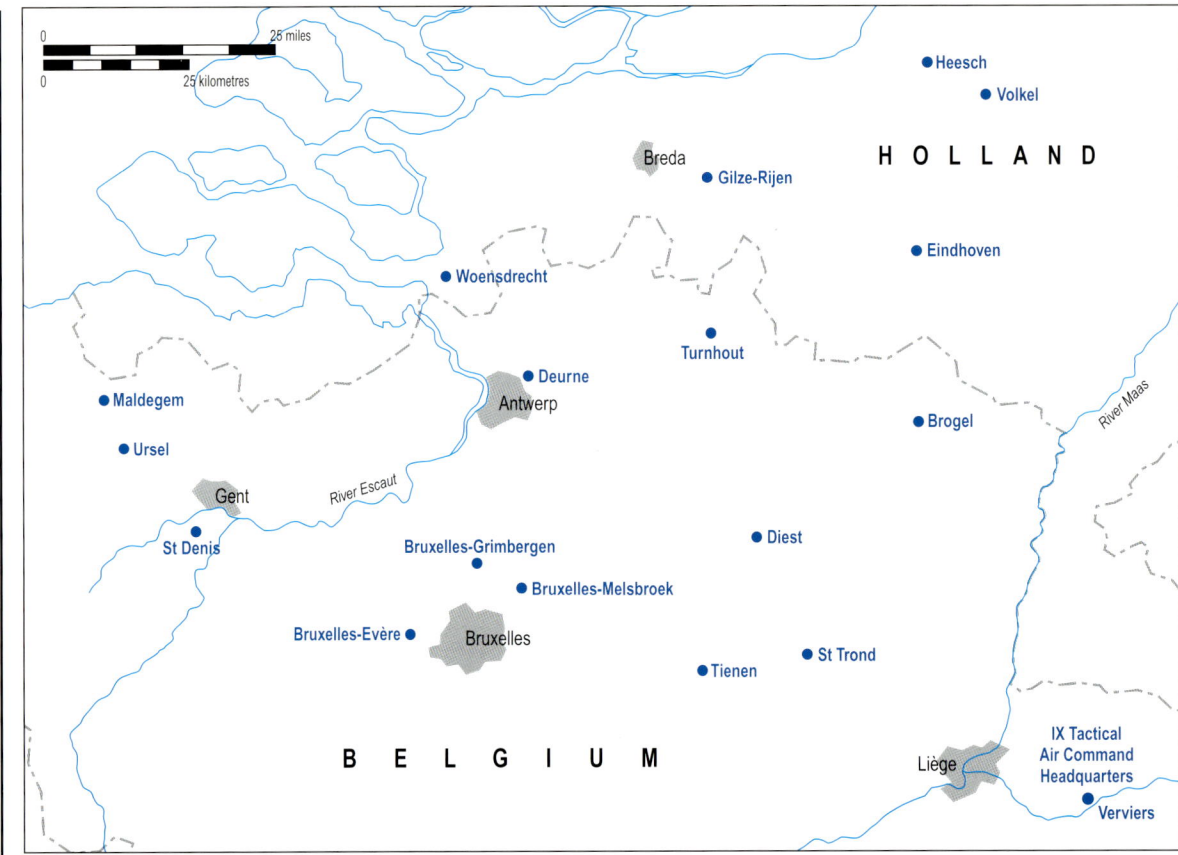

Principal Ninth US Army Air Force airfields used in support of First Army.

there were only three missions flown here, all in front of Patton's Third Army and none of which reported anything significant. Flights over the Monschau region, which might have revealed the German build-up, were disallowed because they could have similarly revealed the Allied intentions regarding the Rur and Urft dams, and in this sense First Army was hoist on its own petard.

The main U.S. Army Air Forces' successes during the battle were not so much over the front line, particularly during the first week, as further to the east, where their disruption of supply trains had a crippling effect on the German intentions, resulting in delay after delay which gave the Allied ground forces time to redeploy to meet the threat. The low clouds which made tactical fighter-bomber operations hazardous or impossible did not hinder the highflying aircraft of Brigadier-General Samuel Anderson's IX Bombardment Command, or UK-based Eighth Air Force B-17s and RAF Lancasters, whose radar enabled them to bomb railway marshalling yards, bridges, airfields and similar strategic targets almost regardless of the weather.

The specific effect of strategic bombing on the course of the battle is impossible to quantify, but one obvious side effect was that many of the fighters of II Jagdkorps assigned to support Sixth Panzer Armee were kept too busy on interception missions to play any really significant part in the battle on the ground. This had a roll-on effect in 1945 when the Allies reached and crossed the Rhine because so many German fighters were lost, especially over the Christmas period, that Adolf Galland called the Ardennes offensive the 'death blow' of the Luftwaffe. The reverse of that coin is that, on occasion, the Allied bombers did suffer heavily. During one raid by B-26s of the 391st Bomb Group, 99th Combat Bomb Wing, on the rail bridge at Ahrweiler, for example, 18 out of 36 Invaders were shot down.

Interdiction attacks against targets west of the Rhine began on 18 December and continued virtually without pause throughout the battle. On 23 December, for example, IX Bombardment Command and Eighth Air Force bombers based in England dropped 1,300 tons of bombs on railways and marshalling yards as well as attacking several bridges. Bridges, however, were difficult targets for high-altitude attacks and, being sturdily built, could often be repaired quite quick-

P-47 Thunderbolts carrying bombs or rockets were the workhorses of IX Tactical Air Command alongside P-38 Lightnings.
(U.S. Air Force)

ly. Eight rail bridges across the Rhine were attacked during the first ten days of the offensive, for example, but five were operational again within 24 hours. It was estimated, in fact, that it took an average of 250 tons of bombs to destroy a metal bridge. However, the effect of the bombing was cumulative, stretching German manpower and resources to their limits. Attacks on rail bridges over the Rivers Ahr, Moselle and Nette in the week preceding the Allied counter-attack in January were more successful: eight out of nine were so seriously damaged that it took an average of five days to get even six of them operational again.

Choke points on the railway lines themselves were also attacked and, although these could usually be repaired quite quickly, in the interim all the supplies in the rail wagons had to be transferred to trucks, itself a time-consuming process, followed by a crawl along the narrow, congested roads to the front line. Time after time the Panzer kampfgruppen had to put off planned attacks until fuel reached them, and even when it did, it was often insufficient to refuel all the vehicles in a column so that attacks had to be launched piecemeal, as in the case of 2 SS-Panzer Division at Manhay.

Allied air attacks on the road network were less effective. IX Bombardment Command aircraft dropped 136 tons of bombs on St Vith without slowing the German traffic at all. Even a subsequent raid, during which the RAF dropped 1,140 tons on the same target, only disrupted the road network for 24 hours. However, when the roads were more constricted by the terrain, some operations were highly effective. On Christmas Eve for example, during the evacuation of

the St Vith salient when CCA of 7th Armored Division was defending the northerly escape route through Vielsalm, at Poteau, a flight of P-38 Lightnings from the 370th Fighter Group, 70th Fighter Wing, caught 9 SS-Panzer Division's leading kampfgruppe forming up to attack and were so successful in strafing and bombing the column in the narrow valley that the German commander had to cancel the assault. On occasion, unfortunately, the Ninth Air Force pilots and navigators did make mistakes.

On Christmas Eve, again, a convoy of 16 German ambulances travelling east from Houffalize, with red crosses clearly marked on their roofs, was strafed by a flight of Lightnings. Even worse happened at Malmédy. On 23 December B-26s of the IX Bombardment Command on a sortie against Zulpich got lost and six of them dropped 86 250lb bombs on the town, killing at least 37 Americans. Disaster followed disaster, because on Christmas Eve, while engineers were still digging survivors from the first raid out of the rubble, a squadron of 18 B-24 Liberators from the Eighth Air Force unloaded their bombs on the town, completely flattening the centre. Nor was that the end, for on Christmas Day itself four B-26s got lost en route to St Vith and again bombed Malmédy by mistake.

But such tragedies, although they had happened before in Normandy, were fortunately rare and, by and large, the Allied air forces did a superb job under often very difficult conditions to support First Army operations and hinder the enemy at every turn. They did not 'win' the battle, since no ground battle can ever be won by air power alone, but they did provide that miraculous 48 hours.

WARGAMING THE ARDENNES
ALLIED NORTHERN SECTOR

Exactly those factors which made the battle in the Ardennes difficult to fight make it difficult to wargame. Mechanised units must stick to roads or valleys, for example, which means that constructing the terrain features accurately is vital. Simple streams, easily fordable by infantry, are usually steep-sided and impassable to armour, so engineers – usually neglected in wargames – are essential to both sides. And there are numerous genuine accounts of platoons, companies and even whole battalions losing their way in the forests.

Now add to this the real 'fog of war': the fact that most engagements either took place at night or in thick ground mist at dawn and dusk. How, as a wargamer, do you recreate this with any realism when you can see all your own and your opponent's pieces neatly arrayed on the table?

The only answer, I suggest, is an umpire and some surrogate players. The two opponents, or teams of opponents, sit in separate rooms and position their forces on maps, which are given to the umpire. He/she then places the playing pieces on the wargames table, but introduces an element of delay here, or faulty map-reading there, so not all the pieces are in exactly the planned places. (This does need an experienced umpire whom all players trust not to play favourites.) Now the surrogate players take their places and respond to orders issued from the respective main players' CPs. If a unit is not in the right place, the order may make no sense and will have to be queried before any movement takes place; or, it may attack 'the hill to the northeast' but choose the wrong one. Only the umpire can decide at what point the opposing forces become visible to each other, and then relay that information back to the main players – whose reaction, as in real life, may well be 'Oh, Hell!'

SELECT BIBLIOGRAPHY

Cole, Hugh M. *The Ardennes: Battle of the Bulge.* United States Army in World War II, Office of the Chief of Military History, Washington D.C., 1965,

Crookenden, Lieutenant-General Sir Napier. *Battle of the Bulge 1944.* Ian Allan, Shepperton, 1980.

Eisenhower, John S.D. *The Bitter Woods.* Robert Hale, London, 1969.

Elstob, Peter. *Hitler's Last Offensive,* Secker & Warburg, London, 1971.

MacDonald, Charles B. *The Battle of the Bulge.* George Weidenfeld & Nicolson, London, 1984.

Pallud, Jean Paul, *Battle of the Bulge Then and Now.* Battle of Britain Prints International, London, 1984.

Parker, Danny S. *Battle of the Bulge.* Greenhill Books, Lionel Leventhal Ltd, London, 1991.

Stanton, Shelby L. *World War II Order of Battle.* Presidio Press, Novato, California, 1984.

Quarrie, Bruce. *Airborne Assault.* Patrick Stephens, Wellingborough, 1991.

Strawson, John. *The Battle for the Ardennes.* B.T. Batsford, London, 1972.

Strong, Major-General Sir Kenneth. *Intelligence at the Top.* Cassell, London, 1968.